Thirteen Modern
English and American
Short Stories

Dans la même collection :

Collection « Lire en anglais »
dirigée par Henri Yvinec

Thirteen Modern English and American Short Stories

Ray Bradbury • Truman Capote • Roald Dahl •
Graham Greene • John Updike • Iain Crichton Smith
• Mary Webb • Somerset Maugham •
Bernard Malamud • Richard Hughes •
Liam O' Flaherty • O. Henry • Katherine Mansfield

Choix et annotations par Henri Yvinec

Le Livre de Poche

Sommaire

Abbreviations

sb.: somebody
sth.: something
fam.: familiar
Am.: American

© *A Piece of Wood:* Ray Bradbury, from *Collected Short Stories*
Mr. Jones: 1975, 1977, 1979, 1980 by Truman Capote, from *Music for Cameleons*,
reprinted by permission of Random House Inc.
The Landlady: 1959 by Roald Dahl, from *Kiss, Kiss*
Dear Alexandros: 1954 by John Updike, from *Pigeon Feathers and Other Short Stories*
by John Updike, by permission of Alfred Knopf Inc.
I Spy: 1930 by Graham Greene. First published in *Twenty One Stories*
The Telegram: Iain Crichton Smith, from *The Black and the Red*, by permission of
Victor Gollancz Ltd.
The Luncheon: The Royal Literary Fund
The Letter: 1968, 1972, 1973, by Bernard Malamud
A Night at a Cottage: Richard Hughes, by permission of David Higham Associated Ltd.
Charity: Liam O' Flaherty by permission of Intercontinental Literary Agency.

Tout naturellement, après quelques années d'étude d'une langue étrangère, naît l'envie de découvrir sa littérature. Mais, par ailleurs, le vocabulaire dont on dispose est souvent insuffisant. La perspective de recherches lexicales multipliées chez le lecteur isolé, la présentation fastidieuse du vocabulaire, pour le professeur, sont autant d'obstacles redoutables. C'est pour tenter de les aplanir que nous proposons cette nouvelle collection.

Celle-ci constitue une étape vers la lecture autonome, sans dictionnaire ni traduction, grâce à des notes facilement repérables. S'agissant des élèves de lycée, les ouvrages de cette collection seront un précieux instrument pédagogique pour les enseignants en langues étrangères puisque les recommandations pédagogiques officielles (Bulletin officiel de l'Éducation nationale du 9 juillet 1987) les invitent à "faire de l'entraînement à la lecture individuelle une activité régulière" qui pourra aller jusqu'à une heure hebdomadaire. Ces recueils de textes devraient ainsi servir de complément à l'étude de la civilisation.

Le lecteur trouvera donc :

En page de gauche

Des textes contemporains choisis pour leur intérêt littéraire et la qualité de leur langue.

En page de droite

Des notes juxtalinéaires rédigées dans la langue du texte, qui aident le lecteur à

Comprendre

Tous les mots et expressions difficiles contenus dans la ligne de gauche sont reproduits en caractères gras et expliqués dans le contexte.

Observer

Des notes d'observation de la langue soulignent le caractère idiomatique de certaines tournures ou constructions.

Apprendre

Dans un but d'enrichissement lexical, certaines notes proposent enfin des synonymes, des antonymes, des expressions faisant appel aux mots qui figurent dans le texte.

Grammaire au fil des nouvelles

Chaque nouvelle est suivie de phrases de thème inspirées du texte avec références à celui-ci pour le corrigé. En les traduisant le lecteur, mis sur la voie par des italiques et/ou des amorces d'explication, révise les structures rebelles les plus courantes ; cette petite "grammaire en contexte" est fondée sur la fréquence des erreurs.

Vocabulaire en contexte

En fin de volume une liste d'un millier de mots contenus dans les nouvelles, suivis de leur traduction, comporte, entre autres, les verbes irréguliers et les mots qui n'ont pas été annotés faute de place ou parce que leur sens était évident dans le contexte. Grâce à ce lexique on pourra, en dernier recours, procéder à quelques vérifications ou faire un bilan des mots retenus au cours des lectures.

A PIECE OF WOOD

by Ray Bradbury (born in 1920)

Ray Bradbury was born in Illinois. He started his own Science-Fantasy magazine at the age of seventeen. After leaving High School he took up a number of jobs, including acting, to support himself while writing. His most famous works are *The Martian Chronicles* (1950), *The Illustrated Man* (1951), *The Golden Apples of the Sun* (1953), *Fahrenheit 451* (1953). The Collected Short Stories are available in Granada Publishers.

Ray Bradbury has his own definition of science-fiction; in his view it is "the sociological study of the future, things that the writer believes are going to happen". Thus real problems are dealt with in his stories: the influence of scientific development upon man, the contradictions between the needs of individuals and the cold indifference of technological society... The values advocated by Ray Bradbury are goodness, innocence, intelligence, beauty. There is often a delicate and poetic touch to his writings.

"Sit down, young man," said the Official.

"Thanks." The young man sat.

"I've been hearing rumours about you," the Official said pleasantly. "Oh, nothing much. Your nervousness. Your not getting on so well. Several months now I've heard about you, and I thought I'd call you in. Thought maybe you'd like your job changed. Like to go overseas, work in some other War Area? Desk job killing you off, like to get right in on the old fight?"

10 "I don't think so," said the young sergeant.

"What *do* you want?"

The sergeant shrugged and looked at his hands. "To live in peace. To learn that during the night, somehow, the guns of the world had rusted, the bacteria had turned sterile in their bomb casings, the tanks had sunk like prehistoric monsters into roads suddenly made tar pits. That's what I'd like."

"That's what we'd all like, of course," said the Official. "Now stop all that idealistic chatter and tell me where you'd 20 like to be sent. You have your choice —the Western or Northern War Zone." The Official tapped a pink map on his desk.

But the sergeant was talking at his hands, turning them over, looking at the fingers: "What would you officers do, what would we men do, what would the *world* do if we all woke tomorrow with the guns in flaking ruin?"

The Official saw that he would have to deal carefully with the sergeant. He smiled quietly. "That's an interesting question. I like to talk about such theories, and my answer 30 is that there'd be mass panic. Each nation would think itself the only unarmed nation in the world, and would blame its enemies for the disaster. There'd be waves of

10

Official: person in authority; the official in charge of..., responsible for... (notice the preposition for)

rumours: all sorts of rumours are going round

nothing much: nothing really important

your not getting...: the fact that you are not so well

call you in: ask you to come and see me, summon you

(I) thought maybe (perhaps) you would like to do (sth.) else

overseas: far away □ **War:** ≠ peace □ **Area:** zone □ (Is) **desk job** (office work) no good for you? □ (would you) **like to get right in on** (directly, in the middle of) **the old fight** (the war that has been going on for years); fight, fought, fought

shrugged: (his shoulders) to express doubt, indifference; shoulder, part of body joining arm to trunk □ **somehow:** in some way

gun(s): cannon □ **world:** universe □ **rusted:** had been corroded by rust □ **casing(s):** covering, container □ **sunk** (deep): gone down slowly (like ships in water) □ **made tar pits:** changed, "turned" into pits (holes, openings) full of (black) tar (asphalt)

chatter: quick, incessant talk about unimportant things

you have your choice: you can choose, select; make a choice

tapped (quickly with his hand) □ **pink:** pale red □ **map:** (geography) showing where countries are □ (writing) **desk** (in office)

at: expresses aggressiveness (he has to use his hands to kill other men, to put them to death) □ there are five **fingers** on each hand

men: soldiers (of lower rank as opposed to officers)

woke: stopped sleeping □ **flaking:** falling off, peeling

deal with: treat, handle □ **carefully:** with care, attention

smiled: had a happy expression showing amusement □ **quietly:** without excitement or noise, discreetly

mass panic, mass meeting... (everybody would panic; to panic)

unarmed: without arms or weapons

waves: the number of suicides would go up (waves of sea)

suicide, stocks collapsing, a million tragedies."

"But *after* that," the sergeant said. "After they realized it was true, that every nation was disarmed and there was nothing more to fear, if we were all clean to start over fresh and new, what then?"

"They'd rearm as swiftly as possible."

"What if they could be stopped?"

"Then they'd beat each other with their fists. If it got down to that. Huge armies of men with boxing gloves of 10 steel pikes would gather at the national borders. And if you took the gloves away they'd use their fingernails and feet. And if you cut their legs off they'd *spit* on each other. And if you cut off their tongues and stopped their mouths with corks they'd fill the atmosphere so full of hate that mosquitoes would drop to the ground and birds would fall dead from telephone wires."

"Then you don't think it would do any good?" the sergeant said.

"Certainly not. It'd be like ripping the carapace off a 20 turtle. Civilization would gasp and die from shock."

The young man shook his head. "Or are you lying to yourself and me because you've a nice comfortable job?"

"Let's call it ninety per cent cynicism, ten per cent rationalizing the situation. Go put your Rust away and forget about it."

The sergeant jerked his head up. "How'd you know I *had* it?" he said.

"Had what?"

"The Rust, of course."

30 "What're you talking about?"

"I *can* do it, you know. I could start the Rust tonight if I wanted to."

12

stocks: *valeurs (en bourse)* ☐ **collapsing:** falling suddenly and completely, dropping dramatically, dropping sharply

true: real ≠ false; speak the truth ≠ tell lies

fear: be afraid of, dread ☐ **...clean to start over...:** pure, immaculate... ready to start a new life; clean ≠ dirty

swiftly: rapidly, quickly, fast

what if...: what would happen if they could be stopped?

fist(s): firmly-closed hand (of boxer) ☐ **if it got down to...:** if that happened ☐ **huge:** immense ☐ **gloves** (on their hands)

steel pikes: pointed pieces of hard metal ☐ **gather...borders:** would assemble at the frontiers ☐ **fingernail(s):** hard end of finger

spit: send liquid (saliva) out from the mouth

tongue(s): organ in the mouth ☐ **stopped:** obstructed, blocked

cork(s) (used to "stop" bottles with) ☐ **hate:** hatred ≠ love

mosquito(es): small flying insects ☐ **ground:** surface of land, soil, earth ☐ **wire(s):** long thin metal cord

do good: ≠ do harm; I'm doing this for your own good

ripping...: cutting, tearing quickly ☐ **off a...:** from a...

turtle: *tortue* ☐ **gasp:** take in air, breathe with difficulty

shook his head (in disapproval) ☐ **lying:** a liar lies

comfortable: (here) with a good pay

let's call it...: let us say it is ninety *per* cent...

rationalizing: finding reasons ☐ **go (and) put away:** put (sth.) away (into a cupboard, on a shelf... where it is usually kept)

jerked: jerk, give a jerk (a sudden quick movement); jerked his head up, suddenly lifted (raised) his head ☐ **how (did) you know I had it** (at all)?... *que je l'avais (seulement)*

of course: naturally (it goes without saying)

what are you talking about?: notice the position of about

I *can* do it: notice the use of italics for emphasis

if I wanted to (start...): notice the omission of the verb

The Official laughed. "You can't be serious."

"I am. I've been meaning to come talk to you. I'm glad you called me in. I've worked on this invention for a long time. It's been a dream of mine. It has to do with the structure of certain atoms. If you study them you find that the arrangement of atoms in steel armour is such-and-such an arrangement. I was looking for an imbalance factor. I majored in physics and metallurgy, you know. It came to me, there's a Rust factor in the air all 10 the time. Water vapour. I had to find a way to give steel a "nervous breakdown." Then the water vapour every-where in the world would take over. Not on all metal, of course. Our civilization is built on steel, I wouldn't want to destroy most buildings. I'd just eliminate guns and shells, tanks, planes, battleships. I can set the machine to work on copper and brass and aluminium, too, if necessary. I'd just walk by all of those weapons and just being near them I'd make them fall away."

The Official was bending over his desk, staring at the 20 sergeant. "May I ask you a question?"

"Yes."

"Have you ever thought you were Christ?"

"I can't say that I have. But I have considered that God was good to me to let me find what I was looking for, if that's what you mean."

The Official reached into his breast pocket and drew out an expensive ball-point pen capped with a rifle shell. He flourished the pen and started filling in a form. "I want you to take this to Dr. Mathews this afternoon, for a 30 complete check-up. Not that I expect anything really bad, understand. But don't you feel you *should* see a doctor?"

"You think I'm lying about my machine," said the

14

laughed (to show how sceptical he was)

I've been meaning to...: it was my intention to, I intended to

glad: pleased and happy; I'm glad of it, I'm glad about that

dream: (sth.) imagined and desired □ **it has to do with**: it has a connection with, it is connected with □ **find**: discover

armour: protective metal covering on tanks... □ **such...**: in a given order □ **looking for**: trying to find □ **imbalance**: ≠ equilibrium □ **I majored...**: I specialized in physics at university

it came to me: the idea came to me, it occurred to me

way: method, means

a nervous breakdown (which you have if you work or worry too much) □ **take over**: do the rest in its turn

built on: based on; build (a house...), built, built

shells fired from gun, (air) **planes, battleships**, warships □ **set...**: make the machine work □ **copper and brass**: *cuivre rouge et cuivre jaune* □ **by**: near

being: by just being there □ **fall away**: disappear, vanish

bending: bend, bent, bent (become curved), bow, stoop □ **staring at...**: looking fixedly with wide-open eyes at...

have you ever thought...: no I have *never* thought...

God: supernatural being who can control everything

good to me: kind to me (to!) □ **to let me find**: to allow or enable me to find □ **what you mean**: what you want to say

reached: (his hand)... □ **breast pocket**: *poche intérieure*

ball-point pen: ≠ fountain pen □ **capped**: with a top (cap) in the shape of a bullet; rifle, gun fired from shoulder □ **flourished**: brandished □ **form**: printed paper with blanks to fill in

check-up: complete medical examination □ **bad**: serious (illness...)

understand: don't get me wrong □ **feel**: have the impression, have a feeling that...

sergeant. "I'm not. It's so small it can be hidden in this cigarette package. The effect of it extends for nine hundred miles. I could tour this country in a few days, with the machine set to a certain type of steel. The other nations couldn't take advantage of us because I'd rust their weapons as they approach us. Then I'd fly to Europe. By this time next month the world would be free of war forever. I don't know how I found this invention. It's impossible. Just as impossible as the 10 atom bomb. I've waited a month now, trying to think it over. I worried about what would happen if I did rip off the carapace, as you say. But now I've just decided. My talk with you has helped clarify things. Nobody thought an aeroplane would ever fly, nobody thought an atom would ever explode, and nobody thinks that there can ever be Peace, but there *will* be."

"Take that paper over to Dr. Mathews, will you?" said the Official hastily.

The sergeant got up. "You're not going to assign me to 20 any new Zone then?"

"Not right away, no. I've changed my mind. We'll let Mathews decide."

"I've decided then," said the young man. "I'm leaving the post within the next few minutes. I've a pass. Thank you very much for giving me your valuable time, sir."

"Now look here, Sergeant, don't take things so seriously. You don't have to leave. Nobody's going to hurt you."

"That's right. Because nobody would believe 30 me. Goodbye, sir." The sergeant opened the office door and stepped out.

The door shut and the Official was alone. He stood for

so small (that...) □ **hidden:** kept unseen; hide, hid, hidden
package (Am.): packet □ **extends:** can be felt as far as...
mile(s): 1,609 m □ **tour:** visit (a country, usually as a tourist); go
on a tour to Italy, go on a cycling tour
take advantage of: triumph over, get the better of
approach us: no preposition! □ **fly,** flew, flown (by plane)
by: not later than □ **time:** period □ **next:** following □ **free of
war:** without war; make free, liberate □ **forever:** always, for all
times, (stronger) for ever and ever
trying: making an effort, an attempt □ **think it over:** consider it
seriously □ **I worried:** I was anxious □ **happen:** take place,
occur
talk: conversation □ **has helped clarify things:** help + verb without
to or with to: will you be good enough to help me (to) do this?

peace: be at peace with (sb.); make one's peace with (sb.)
Dr. Mathews, President Reagan, Queen Elizabeth...: no articles!
hastily: rapidly, in haste; make haste, hurry up
assign: appoint to (a post, a job...)

right away: immediately □ **I've changed my mind:** I've changed my
intention (opinion, purpose)
I'm leaving: I'll be leaving; leave, left, left; quit, give up
within: in less than; within an hour □ **pass:** safe-conduct
valuable: of great value □ **sir:** used by soldiers speaking to
officers □ **look here:** (listen!) used to draw sb's attention
you don't have to leave (to go) nobody asks you to (p. 14, l. 10)
hurt you: do you any harm (≠ do good); hurt, hurt, hurt
right: correct □ **believe:** accept as true; believe in God
office: an office is a room, a desk is a piece of furniture
stepped out: walked out; step, take a step (movement of the foot
in walking) □ **alone:** with nobody else, by himself

a moment looking at the door. He sighed. He rubbed his hands over his face. The phone rang. He answered it abstractedly.

"Oh, *hello,* Doctor. I was just going to call you." A pause. "Yes, I was going to send him over to you. Look, is it all right for that young man to be wandering about? It *is* all right? If you say so, Doctor. Probably needs a rest, a good long one. Poor boy has a delusion of rather an interesting sort. Yes, yes. It's a shame. But that's what 10 a Sixteen-Year War can do to you, I suppose."

The phone voice buzzed in reply.

The Official listened and nodded. "I'll make a note on that. Just a second." He reached for his ball-point pen. "Hold on a moment. Always mislaying things." He patted his pocket. "Had my pen here a moment ago. Wait." He put down the phone and searched his desk, pulling out drawers. He checked his blouse pocket again. He stopped moving. Then his hands twitched slowly into his pocket and probed 20 down. He poked his thumb and forefinger deep and brought out a pinch of something.

He sprinkled it on his desk blotter: a small filtering powder of yellow-red rust.

He sat staring at it for a moment. Then he picked up the phone. "Mathews," he said, "get off the line, quick." There was a click of someone hanging up and then he dialled another call. "Hello, Guard Station, listen, there's a man coming past you any minute now, you know him, name of Sergeant Hollis, stop him, shoot him down, 30 kill him if necessary, don't ask questions, kill the son of a bitch, you heard me, this is the Official talking! Yes, kill him, you hear!"

sighed: gave a sigh (*soupir*) □ **rubbed:** rub, move (sth.) backwards and forwards on the surface of (sth.) else □ **rang:** could be heard ringing; ring, rang, rung □ **abstractedly:** abstracted, inattentive to what is happening, lost in thought □ **call you** on the phone, phone you, ring you up □ **send** (for a "check-up") □ **is it all right for...to:** is there any problem, danger if □ **wandering about:** going here and there when he likes □ **so:** if you say so, if you say it is all right □ **a rest:** a break (after work) □ **delusion:** illusion □ **rather:** quite **a shame:** (sth.) regrettable; it's a shame, it's a pity

buzzed: made a buzz, a low confused sound □ **reply:** answer **nodded** (his head), showing he agreed □ **make a note...:** (not do!): write down

hold on: wait (on the phone) □ **mislay(ing):** put (sth.) in a place and forget where □ **patted:** hit gently with the hand

put down the phone: (receiver on his desk)

searched: examined □ **drawer(s):** box-like container □ **checked:** made sure it was not in his **blouse** (U.S. Army jacket) pocket

twitched: moved nervously, uncontrollably □ **probed:** explored **poked** (pushed) his **thumb** (*pouce*), **forefinger** (*index*) **deep**(ly) (profoundly) □ **pinch:** quantity held between thumb and finger

sprinkled: dropped, spread □ **desk-blotter:** *sous-main* □ **filtering:** filter, pass through □ **powder:** fine substance; talcum powder

staring: looking fixedly with wide open eyes □ **picked up the phone:** ≠ put down the phone □ **get off the line:** put down the receiver **quick**(ly), immediately □ **hanging up** (Am.): ringing off

dialled: to get the police dial 999; a telephone call

any minute (from) now: he's expected to come any time now

shoot: hurt or kill (sb.) with a gun, a rifle...; he was shot in the leg; shoot (sb.) to death, kill (sb.) (with a gun...) □ **the son of a bitch:** (insult) bastard!; bitch, bad woman

"But sir," said a bewildered voice on the other end of the line. "I can't, I just *can't*..."

"What do you mean, you can't, God damn it!"

"Because..." the voice faded away. You could hear the guard breathing into the phone a mile away.

The Official shook the phone. "Listen to me, listen, get your gun ready!"

"I can't shoot anyone," said the guard.

The Official sank back in his chair. He sat blinking for
10 half a minute, gasping.

Out there even now —he didn't have to look, no one had to tell him— the hangars were dusting down in soft red rust, and the aeroplanes were blowing away on a brown-rust wind into nothingness, and the tanks were sinking, sinking slowly into the hot asphalt roads, like dinosaurs (isn't that what the man had said?) sinking into primordial tar pits. Trucks were blowing away in ochre puffs of smoke, their drivers dumped by the road, with only the tyres left running on the highways.

20 "Sir..." said the guard, who was seeing all this, far away. "Oh, God..."

"Listen, listen!" screamed the Official. "Go after him, get him, with your hands, choke him, with your fists, beat him, use your feet, kick his ribs in, kick him to death, do anything, but get that man. I'll be right out!" He hung up the phone.

By instinct he jerked open the bottom desk drawer to get his service pistol. A pile of brown rust filled the new leather holster. He swore and leaped up.

30 On the way out of the office he grabbed a chair. It's wood, he thought. Good old-fashioned wood, good old-fashioned maple. He hurled it against the wall twice, and

bewildered: perplexed, confused, puzzled

I can't: the "Rust" is "set to work" on his gun, corroding, "rusting" the metal □ **God damn it!:** good God! (bloody) hell!

faded away: could be heard less and less, died away

breathing: breathe, take in air; breath, respiration

shook (impatiently, angrily); shake, shook, shaken, move (sth.) up and down and side to side

sank back: let himself go, dropped, collapsed □ **blinking:** shutting and opening his eyes quickly

even now: at this very instant, right now

dusting down: falling, turning into dust (*poussière*) □ **soft:** pale ≠ bright □ **blowing away...:** carried away on a brown-rust

wind (*vent*), disappearing, vanishing..., reduced to nothing

slowly: little by little, gradually ≠ suddenly, all of a sudden

primordial: existing from the beginning of time, original

truck(s) (Am.): lorry, large vehicle □ **puff(s):** short quick breath of smoke, wind... □ **dumped:** deposited, dropped □ **tyre:** pneumatic tyre □ **highway(s):** (important) main road

far away: a long way away, in the distance

screamed: cried out on a high note □ **go after:** chase (him)

get: (slang) kill □ **choke:** suffocate, strangle, throttle

kick: hit with the foot; kick in, break... □ **rib(s):** *côte*

right: directly, straight (right now, immediately)

he jerked open...: he suddenly opened... □ **bottom desk:** ≠ top desk

service: the armed Services (Army...) □ **filled:** made full

holster: pistol case made of **leather** □ **swore...leaped:** used bad language (God damn), stood up abruptly □ **grabbed:** seized

wood (from a tree trunk) □ **old-fashioned:** of olden days

maple: tree associated with Canada □ **hurled:** threw violently

21

it broke.   Then he seized one of the legs, clenched it hard in his fist, his face bursting red, the breath snorting in his nostrils, his mouth wide.   He struck the palm of his hand with the leg of the chair, testing it.   "All right, God damn it, come on!" he cried.

He rushed out, yelling, and slammed the door.

clenched it hard: held it tightly (firmly)

bursting: exploding (with anger) □ **snorting:** like a pig taking in air through the **nostrils** □ **wide** open □ **struck:** hit

testing it: making sure he could use it as a weapon

come on: (persuading himself) let's go!

rushed out: hurried out □ **yelling:** giving a loud cry □ **slammed the door:** shut it violently

Grammaire au fil des nouvelles

Traduisez les phrases suivantes inspirées du texte (le premier chiffre renvoie aux pages, les suivants aux lignes) :

... Oh, pas grand-chose, le fait que vous ne vous portez pas tellement bien... (gérondif, 10.5).

Il comprit qu'*il lui faudrait* traiter le sergent avec prudence (substituts des auxiliaires modaux, 10.27).

Il y aurait la panique générale (10.30).

Ils se battraient à coups de poing (réciprocité, 12.8).

Si vous leur coupiez la langue, ils rempliraient l'atmosphère de haine... (pluriel des noms désignant un objet... qui n'appartient pas en commun aux différents possesseurs, 12.13).

De quoi parlez-vous ? (rejet de la préposition, 12.30)

Je *travaille* à cette invention *depuis* longtemps (14.3).

Il fallait que je trouve un moyen (auxiliaires modaux et substituts, 14.10).

Avez-vous *jamais* pensé que vous étiez le Christ ? (14.22)

Dieu était bon de me permettre de trouver *ce que* je cherchais (**let** et **make** +...; rejet de la préposition, 14.24).

Je veux que vous portiez ceci au Docteur Mathews (proposition infinitive ; noms de personnes précédés d'un titre, 14.29).

L'effet s'étend à neuf cents miles (**hundred, thousand, dozen** précédés d'un nombre précis, de **a few, several, many**, 16.2).

Je viens de décider (passé immédiat, 16.12).

Je vais quitter le poste dans les quelques minutes qui viennent (expression du futur à la forme progressive, 16.23).

Vous n'avez pas besoin de vous en aller. Personne ne va vous faire de mal (modal : absence d'obligation ; futur proche, 16.27).

Est-ce bien que ce jeune homme circule librement ? (proposition infinitive introduite par **for**, 18.6).

Faites *n'importe* quoi, mais zigouillez cet homme (**some, any, no** et leurs composés, 20.25).

MR. JONES

by Truman Capote (1924-1984)

Truman Capote was born in New Orleans. He spent most of his childhood on a cotton plantation in the South. He started writing short stories at the age of seventeen and travelled throughout the United States doing all sorts of jobs including newspaper reporting for the New Yorker, dancing and painting. His first novel *Other Voices, Other Rooms* was published in 1948 and brought him fame. Another well-known book by him is *In Cold Blood* (1966) which is half-fiction, half-reporting. His collections of short stories are to be found in Penguin Books, Signet Books and New American Library; they are *A Tree of Night and Other Stories, Breakfast at Tiffany's, Music for Cameleons...*

Truman Capote's novels and short stories have often a Southern quality about them. His characters are delightfully unconventional people like *Mr. Jones,* lonely old ladies with "six or seven cats" like the heroine of *A Lamp in a Window* (both stories included in *Music for Cameleons*). His style, pleasantly precious, is remarkable for its clarity.

During the winter of 1945 I lived for several months in a rooming house in Brooklyn. It was not a shabby place, but a pleasantly furnished, elderly brownstone kept hospital-neat by its owners, two maiden sisters.

Mr. Jones lived in the room next to mine. My room was the smallest in the house, his the largest, a nice big sunshiny room, which was just as well, for Mr. Jones never left it: all his needs, meals, shopping, laundry, were attended to by the middle-aged landladies. Also, he was not without visitors; on the average, a half-dozen various persons, men and women, young, old, in-between, visited his room each day, from early morning until late in the evening. He was not a drug dealer or a fortuneteller; no, they came just to talk to him and apparently they made him small gifts of money for his conversation and advice. If not, he had no obvious means of support.

I never had a conversation with Mr. Jones myself, a circumstance I've often since regretted. He was a handsome man, about forty. Slender, black-haired, and with a distinctive face; a pale, lean face, high cheekbones, and with a birthmark on his left cheek, a small scarlet defect shaped like a star. He wore gold-rimmed glasses with pitch-black lenses: he was blind, and crippled, too—according to the sisters, the use of his legs had been denied him by a childhood accident, and he could not move without crutches. He was always dressed in a crisply pressed dark grey or blue three-piece suit and a subdued tie—as though about to set off for a Wall Street office.

However, as I've said, he never left the premises. Simply sat in his cheerful room in a comfortable chair and received visitors. I had no notion of why they came to see him, these rather ordinary-looking folk, or what

winter (season) ☐ **January** is the first **month** of the year
rooming house (Am.): lodging house ☐ **shabby**: in bad repair
furnished: *meublé* ☐ **elderly**: old ☐ **brownstone** (house): *grès de construction* ☐ **neat**: clean ☐ **owner(s)**: proprietor ☐ **maiden**: unmarried ☐ **next to mine**: near mine; adjoining room(s)
sunshiny: with plenty of sunshine; the sun shines bright
for: because ☐ **never left it**: never went out of it; to leave
meals (lunch...) **laundry** (clothes to wash)... **attended to** (looked after) ☐ **middle-aged**: neither old nor young ☐ **landladies** keep lodging houses ☐ **on the average, a half-dozen** (six), sometimes more sometimes less ☐ **in-between**: "middle-aged"

drug dealer: trafficker ☐ **a fortuneteller** tells the future
gift(s): present; give, gave, given
advice: opinion about how to act ☐ **obvious**: visible, evident
means of support like a job, money to live on, financial means; he has a large family to support (to provide for financially)

handsome: good-looking ☐ **slender**: attractively thin, not fat
lean: meagre, gaunt ☐ **cheekbone(s)**: *pommette*
birthmark, birthday... ☐ **scarlet**: red ☐ **defect**: imperfection
shaped: in the form of ☐ **gold**: precious metal ☐ **rim**: border
pitch-black: very dark ☐ **(contact) lenses** ☐ **blind, crippled**: unable to see, unable to walk ("the use of his legs had been **denied** him by a **childhood** accident when he was a child")
crutch(es) supporting him ☐ **crisply**: neatly
pressed: ironed (*repassé*) ☐ **subdued**: ≠ bright
tie: *cravate* ☐ **as though** (as if he was **about to set off** (on the point of leaving) ☐ **however**: yet, nevertheless ☐ **the premises**: the place, the rooming-house ☐ **(He) simply**: just, only ☐ **cheerful**: ≠ sad, cheerless ☐ **I had no notion** (of) **why**: I had no idea why
folk: people

they talked about, and I was far too concerned with my own affairs to much wonder over it. When I did, I imagined that his friends had found in him an intelligent, kindly man, a good listener in whom to confide and consult with over their troubles: a cross between a priest and a therapist.

Mr. Jones had a telephone. He was the only tenant with a private line. It rang constantly, often after midnight and as early as six in the morning.

I moved to Manhattan. Several months later I returned 10 to the house to collect a box of books I had stored there. While the landladies offered me tea and cakes in their lace-curtained "parlor," I inquired of Mr. Jones.

The women lowered their eyes. Clearing her throat, one said: "It's in the hands of the police.".

The other offered: "We've reported him as a missing person."

The first added: "Last month, twenty-six days ago, my sister carried up Mr. Jones's breakfast, as usual. He wasn't there. All his belongings were there. But he was 20 gone."

"It's odd—"

"—how a man totally blind, a helpless cripple—"

Ten years pass.

Now it is a zero-cold December afternoon, and I am in Moscow. I am riding in a subway car. There are only a few other passengers. One of them is a man sitting opposite me, a man wearing boots, a thick long coat and a Russian-style fur cap. He has bright eyes, blue as a 30 peacock's.

After a doubtful instant, I simply stared, for even without the black glasses, there was no mistaking that lean

28

far too concerned: much too preoccupied ☐ **own:** personal
affairs: problems ☐ **wonder over:** ask myself questions about
kindly: showing sympathy or love for others, kind-hearted
confide in (to) (sb.): tell (sth.) to (sb.) confidentially ☐ **over:** about
troubles: difficulties ☐ **cross:** combination ☐ **priest:** clergyman
tenant: one who occupies one of the landlady's rooms
rang: ring, rang, rung ☐ **midnight:** twelve o'clock at night
early: ≠ late ☐ **at six in the morning:** notice "in"
moved (house): changed address ☐ **several:** more than two
collect: get, take ☐ **stored:** kept, left
while: during the time that
lace: *dentelle* ☐ **curtain:** *rideau* ☐ **parlor:** *salon* ☐ **inquired of:** asked
questions about ☐ **lowered...** (looked down), **cleared her throat**
(*gorge*) in embarrassment not because she had a cold
offered: said, added ☐ **reported** him **as a missing** person: notified,
told the police he was not to be found or seen anywhere
added: add ≠ subtract; addition ≠ subtraction
carried... to his room ☐ **as usual:** as she always did
belongings: personal possession; it belongs to me, it's mine
he was gone: he had disappeared, he was no longer there
odd: strange, unusual; an oddity, a strange person, thing...
helpless: defenceless ☐ **a cripple** (noun!) (p. 26 l. 23)

zero is used for temperatures; ten degrees below zero
riding: travelling ☐ **subway** (Am.): underground ☐ **car** (Am.)
carriage (railway carriage)
boot(s): type of shoe for rain or snow ☐ **thick:** ≠ thin
fur cap: type of hat made of animal's skin ☐ **bright:** shining
a peacock's (eyes): bird with splendid plumage
doubtful: full of doubt ☐ **stared:** looked fixedly (astonished)
there was no mistaking: no possibility of being wrong about

distinctive face, those high cheekbones with the single scarlet star-shaped birthmark.

I was just about to cross the aisle and speak to him when the train pulled into a station, and Mr. Jones, on a pair of fine sturdy legs, stood up and strode out of the car. Swiftly, the train door closed behind him.

single: only, one and only

star-shaped, lace-curtained, long-haired, blue-eyed...

aisle: (Am.) passage between rows (lines) of seats

pulled into a station: entered a station (and stopped)

fine: nice □ **sturdy:** strong □ **strode:** walked with long steps

swiftly: quickly □ **closed:** shut (no reflexive pronouns!)

Grammaire au fil des nouvelles

Traduisez les phrases suivantes inspirées du texte (le premier chiffre renvoie aux pages, les suivants aux lignes) :

Ma pièce était la plus petite de la maison, la sienne la plus grande, *ce qui* était tout aussi bien (26.5).

Tous ses besoins étaient pris en charge par les logeuses d'âge mûr (forme passive des verbes à particule, 26.8).

Il n'était pas trafiquant de drogue ou diseur de bonne aventure (emploi de l'article avec noms attributs, noms de métiers le plus souvent, 26.13).

Il n'avait aucun moyen de subsistance apparent (**some, any, no**, 26.15).

Je n'ai jamais eu une conversation avec Mr. Jones personnellement, *circonstance* que j'ai souvent regrettée depuis (noms en apposition, 26.17).

C'était un homme aux cheveux noirs (adjectifs composés, 26.18).

Il était habillé d'un costume trois-pièces, comme s'il était sur le point de partir pour Wall Street (futur imminent, 26.26).

Je n'avais aucune idée de ce dont ils parlaient (rejet de la préposition, 26.31).

Je retournerai à la maison *pour* prendre une caisse de livres que j'y avais entreposée (pronoms relatifs compléments..., 28.10).

Les femmes baissèrent *les* yeux. S'éclaircissant *la* gorge, l'une d'elles dit... (emploi du possessif devant noms de parties du corps, 28.13).

Le mois dernier, *il y a* vingt-six jours, ma sœur *a porté* le petit déjeuner de Mr. Jones là-haut, comme d'habitude (28.17).

Il n'y a que *peu* d'autres voyageurs. L'un d'eux est un homme assis en face de moi (quantificateurs ; **other** adjectif ou pronom ! positions du corps, 28.26).

Il a des yeux vifs, bleus comme *ceux d'*un paon (28.29).

Il n'y avait pas moyen de se méprendre sur ce visage caractéristique avec l'unique marque de naissance en forme d'étoile (expressions suivies du gérondif, 28.32 ; adjectifs composés, 28.32).

THE LANDLADY

by Roald Dahl (1916-1990)

Roald Dahl was born in Wales of Norwegian parents. During the Second World War he served in the R.A.F. as a fighter pilot and was severely wounded in Libya. In 1942 when he was an Assistant Air Attaché in Washington he began to write short stories *(Over to You)* about his R.A.F. experiences. Many of his stories have been dramatized for television *(Tales of the Unexpected)* and he has written successful children's books like *Charlie and the Chocolate Factory,* all of which have been translated into many languages. His very last book is entitled *Two Fables* (1986. Viking Publisher).

Most of Roald Dahl's collections of short stories are available in Penguin Books: *Completed Unexpected Tales* include *Tales of the Unexpected* and *More Tales of the Unexpected.* Other titles are *Someone Like You, Kiss Kiss* and *Switch Bitch.*

Strange, bizarre, grotesque, alarming and disturbing, macabre, such are the adjectives which most commonly occur to the minds of the critics of the brilliant story-teller, the master of black humour.

Billy Weaver had travelled down from London on the slow afternoon train, with a change at Swindon on the way, and by the time he got to Bath it was about nine o'clock in the evening and the moon was coming up out of a clear starry sky over the houses opposite the station entrance. But the air was deadly cold and the wind was like a flat blade of ice on his cheeks.

"Excuse me," he said, "but is there a fairly cheap hotel not too far away from here?"

10 "Try The Bell and Dragon," the porter answered, pointing down the road. "They might take you in. It's about a quarter of a mile along on the other side."

Billy thanked him and picked up his suitcase and set out to walk the quarter-mile to The Bell and Dragon. He had never been to Bath before. He didn't know anyone who lived there. But Mr. Greenslade at the Head Office in London had told him it was a splendid city. "Find your own lodgings," he had said, "and then go along and report to the Branch Manager as soon as you've got yourself 20 settled."

Billy was seventeen years old. He was wearing a new navy-blue overcoat, a new brown trilby hat, and a new brown suit, and he was feeling fine. He walked briskly down the street. He was trying to do everything briskly these days. Briskness, he had decided, was *the* one common characteristic of all successful businessmen. The big shots up at Head Office were absolutely fantastically brisk all the time. They were amazing.

There were no shops on this wide street that he was 30 walking along, only a line of tall houses on each side, all of them identical. They had porches and pillars and four or five steps going up to their front doors, and it was obvious

travelled: travel light, with little luggage or baggage (Am.)
slow train: stops at every station □ **on the way:** en route
by the time: when □ **got to :** arrived in □ **about:** approximately
moon: the moon shines at night □ **clear:** ≠ dark, cloudy
starry sky: sky full of stars □ **opposite:** in front of
deadly cold: very cold □ **wind:** moving air; the wind blows
flat: *plat* □ **blade:** *lame* □ **ice:** *glace* □ **cheek(s):** side of face below
eye □ **fairly:** moderately □ **cheap:** inexpensive ≠ expensive, costly,
dear
porter: one who carries luggage in a railway station
pointing: showing the direction with his finger
a quarter of a mile: = about 400 m.; 1 mile = 1,609 m.
suitcase: case for carrying things when travelling □ **set out to walk:**
began to walk

the Head Office in London, the most important one, the main
office as opposed to the branch offices in the provinces
report to...: go and tell him you are ready for work
as soon as you've got yourself settled: as soon as you've found
lodgings; I hate all this travel, I want to settle down

navy-blue: very dark blue □ **trilby hat:** *chapeau mou*
suit: jacket and trousers □ **fine:** on form □ **briskly:** quickly and
actively; brisk, quick, energetic, lively, alert
briskness: energy □ **the one...:** the characteristic par excellence
successful: success; succeed in doing (sth.)
big shot(s): (pejorative) important people, V.I.P.'s
amazing: extraordinary; amaze, astonish, astound
wide: ≠ narrow; this street is ten metres wide
a line: a row; a row of identical houses joined to each other is a
"terrace"; the houses are "terraced houses"
front door(s): ≠ back door(s) □ **obvious:** evident, clear

that once upon a time they had been very swanky residences. But now, even in the darkness, he could see that the paint was peeling from the woodwork on their doors and windows, and that the handsome white façades were cracked and blotchy from neglect.

Suddenly, in a downstairs window that was brilliantly illuminated by a street-lamp not six yards away, Billy caught sight of a printed notice propped up against the glass in one of the upper panes. It said BED AND BREAK-
10 FAST. There was a vase of pussy-willows, tall and beautiful, standing just underneath the notice.

He stopped walking. He moved a bit closer. Green curtains (some sort of velvety material) were hanging down on either side of the window. The pussy-willows looked wonderful beside them. He went right up and peered through the glass into the room, and the first thing he saw was a bright fire burning in the hearth. On the carpet in front of the fire, a pretty little dachshund was curled up asleep with its nose tucked into its belly. The room itself,
20 so far as he could see in the half-darkness, was filled with pleasant furniture. There was a baby-grand piano and a big sofa and several plump armchairs; and in one corner he spotted a large parrot in a cage. Animals were usually a good sign in a place like this, Billy told himself; and all in all, it looked to him as though it would be a pretty decent house to stay in. Certainly it would be more comfortable than The Bell and Dragon.

On the other hand, a pub would be more congenial than a boarding-house. There would be beer and darts in the
30 evenings, and lots of people to talk to, and it would probably be a good bit cheaper, too. He had stayed a couple of nights in a pub once before and he had liked it.

once upon a time: some time ago □ **swanky:** (fam.) pretentiously elegant □ **even...:** even if, although it was dark

peeling: coming off in small pieces □ **woodwork:** parts (of doors, windows) made of wood □ **handsome:** good-looking

cracked, blotchy from neglect: with cracks, fissures, with dirty marks (blotches) for being neglected (not well kept)

street lamp: lamp-post □ **yard(s):** 1 yard = 3 feet = 91,44 cm

caught sight...: saw an announcement written in block letters put up... □ **upper:** ≠ lower (top ≠ bottom) □ **panel(s):** division of a window made of glass □ **pussy-willow(s):** *saule blanc*

just underneath: exactly under, right under

he moved a bit closer: he walked a little nearer

curtain(s): cloth or material (here velvet, *velours*) hanging at a window □ **on either side:** on both sides (right and left)

beside: near □ **right:** directly □ **peered:** looked carefully

bright: nice and bright, shining □ **hearth:** part of fireplace

pretty: nice □ **dachshund:** short-legged dog □ **curled up:** like a ball

asleep: sleeping □ **tucked...:** laid comfortably onto its stomach

so far as: *autant que* □ **filled with:** full of

furniture: tables, chairs... □ **baby-grand piano:** small grand (≠ upright) piano □ **plump:** nice and big, deep, comfortable

spotted: saw, noticed □ **parrot:** bird that imitates men speaking

all in all: considering everything

it looked to him as though it would be a pretty decent...: it seemed to him; as though, as if; pretty (fam.) quite, rather; decent, good enough, passable, satisfactory

on the other hand: *par ailleurs* □ **congenial:** attractive

boarding-house: where you can eat and sleep □ **darts:** a very popular game in English pubs □ **to talk to:** to whom to talk

a good bit cheaper: (fam.) much cheaper, much less expensive

a couple of nights: two nights □ **once:** on one occasion

He had never stayed in any boarding-houses, and, to be perfectly honest, he was a tiny bit frightened of them. The name itself conjured up images of watery cabbage, rapacious landladies, and a powerful smell of kippers in the living-room.

After dithering about like this in the cold for two or three minutes, Billy decided that he would walk on and take a look at The Bell and Dragon before making up his mind. He turned to go.

10 And now a queer thing happened to him. He was in the act of stepping back and turning away from the window when all at once his eye was caught and held in the most peculiar manner by the small notice that was there. BED AND BREAKFAST, it said. BED AND BREAKFAST, BED AND BREAKFAST, BED AND BREAKFAST. Each word was like a large black eye staring at him through the glass, holding him, compelling him, forcing him to stay where he was and not to walk away from that house, and the next thing he knew, he was actually moving across from the window to the front door of the 20 house, climbing the steps that led up to it, and reaching for the bell.

He pressed the bell. Far away in a back room he heard it ringing, and then *at once* —it must have been at once because he hadn't even had time to take his finger from the bell-button— the door swung open and a woman was standing there.

Normally you ring the bell and you have at least a half-minute's wait before the door opens. But this dame was like a jack-in-the-box. He pressed the bell —and out she 30 popped! It made him jump.

She was about forty-five or fifty years old, and the

stayed: stay in a boarding-house, put up or stop at a hotel
a tiny bit: (fam.) a little □ **frightened of:** afraid of
conjured up: evoked □ **cabbage:** *chou*
landladies keep boarding-houses □ **powerful:** strong □ **kipper(s):** dried herring *(hareng fumé)*
dithering: (fam.) hesitating nervously
walk on: go on walking, continue walking
making up his mind: making or taking a decision

queer: strange, unusual, odd, peculiar
stepping: walking; a step, a movement of the foot in walking
all at once: suddenly □ **his eye was caught...:** he saw and could not take his eye off the notice (hold, held, held)
bed and breakfast: notice the "printed" words; B and B
each word: every single word □ **large:** big (not wide!) □ **staring at:** looking fixedly at □ **holding:** making him unable to move □ **compelling:** forcing; school is compulsory up to 16 □ **the next thing he knew:** before he realized what he was doing □ **actually:** in fact □ **moving across:** walking, stepping across
climbing: going up □ **step(s):** *marche* □ **led:** all roads lead to Rome
reaching out (his hand or arm) **for the bell,** to be able to press it
back room: ≠ front room
at once: immediately, without delay, there and then

the door swung open: the door opened as if automatically; swing, swung, swung, move from side to side
at least: as a minimum ≠ at the most
wait: wait is a noun here! □ **dame:** (amusingly) lady
jack-in-the-box: box with amusing figure coming out suddenly ("popping out") when top is opened □ **jump** (in surprise), start
about: ≠ exactly, just; forty-five or thereabouts

moment she saw him, she gave him a warm welcoming
smile.

"*Please* come in," she said pleasantly. She stepped
aside, holding the door wide open, and Billy found himself
automatically starting forward into the house. The
compulsion or, more accurately, the desire to follow after
her into that house was extraordinarily strong.

"I saw the notice in the window," he said, holding himself
back.

10   "Yes, I know."

"I was wondering about a room."

"It's *all* ready for you, my dear," she said. She had a
round pink face and very gentle blue eyes.

"I was on my way to The Bell and Dragon," Billy told
her. "But the notice in your window just happened to
catch my eye."

"My dear boy," she said, "why don't you come in out of
the cold?"

"How much do you charge?"

20   "Five and six pence a night, including breakfast."

It was fantastically cheap. It was less than half of what
he had been willing to pay.

"If that is too much," she added, "then perhaps I can
reduce it just a tiny bit. Do you desire an egg for
breakfast? Eggs are expensive at the moment. It would
be sixpence less without the egg."

"Five and six pence is fine," he answered. "I should like
very much to stay here."

"I knew you would. Do come in."

30   She seemed terribly nice. She looked exactly like the
mother of one's best school-friend welcoming one into the

the moment: as soon as ☐ **warm:** ≠ cool ☐ **welcoming:** welcome, show that one is happy when (sb.) arrives ☐ **smile:** happy expression on the face ☐ **pleasantly:** in a friendly manner ☐ **stepped aside** to let him pass ☐ **wide open:** fully open ≠ ajar
forward: ≠ backward
compulsion: the fact of being compelled ☐ **accurately:** exactly; accurate, precise, exact; accuracy, exactness
holding himself back: trying to stop walking (on into the house)

wondering: (I was) asking myself if you had a room

pink: pale red ☐ **gentle:** nice and quiet ≠ violent, rough
I was on my way to...: I was walking in the direction of
happened to catch my eye: caught my attention accidentally, by chance; I happened to see him in the street, it was quite a surprise

how much do you charge?: what is the charge? (the amount of money you ask for the room) ☐ **a night:** for each night, per night; we walked twenty kilometres a day (every day)
he had been willing to pay: he had been prepared or ready to pay
added: add ≠ subtract; addition ≠ subtraction
reduce: reduce the rent (price for room); make a reduction
at the moment: these days, nowadays

five and six pence is fine: five shillings and six pence; 1 shilling = 12 pence (until 1971); fine, alright, perfect
do come in: (emphatic) please come in
looked like: look like (sb.), resemble (sb.) (no preposition!)
one's best school-friend: anybody's friend (generally)

41

house to stay for the Christmas holidays. Billy took off his
hat, and stepped over the threshold.

"Just hang it there," she said, "and let me help you with
your coat."

There were no other hats or coats in the hall. There
were no umbrellas, no walking-sticks —nothing.

"We have it *all* to ourselves," she said, smiling at him over
her shoulder as she led the way upstairs. "You see, it isn't
very often I have the pleasure of taking a visitor into my
10 little nest."

The old girl is slightly dotty, Billy told himself. But at
five and six pence a night, who gives a damn about
that? "I should've thought you'd be simply swamped with
applicants," he said politely.

"Oh, I am, my dear, I am, of course I am. But the
trouble is that I'm inclined to be just a teeny weeny bit
choosy and particular —if you see what I mean."

"Ah, yes."

"But I'm always ready. Everything is always ready day
20 and night in this house just on the off-chance that an
acceptable young gentleman will come along. And it is
such a pleasure, my dear, such a very great pleasure when
now and again I open the door and I see someone standing
there who is just *exactly* right." She was half-way up the
stairs, and she paused with one hand on the stair-rail,
turning her head and smiling down at him with pale
lips. "Like you," she added, and her blue eyes travelled
slowly all the way down the length of Billy's body, to his
feet, and then up again.

30 On the first-floor landing she said to him, "This floor is
mine."

They climbed up a second flight. "And this one is *all*

42

took off: ≠ put on (hat, clothes in general)

threshold: doorstep, entrance

hang: coat hanger ☐ **help me with my coat:** (with!); he often helps his younger brother with his homework

other: (adjective) no s! ≠ give me the other*s* (pronoun!)

umbrellas used in the rain, **walking-sticks** to help old people walk

all...: the whole house just for the two of us

shoulder: part of body joining arm to trunk ☐ **led the way upstairs:** preceded him up the stairs to the bedroom (upstairs ≠ downstairs)

nest: place made by a bird for its eggs

old girl: (amusingly) old lady ☐ **slightly dotty:** a little mad

who gives a damn: who attaches any importance to...? who cares?

simply: absolutely ☐ **be swamped with applicants:** have too many people applying for (asking for) the room; this business-man is swamped with work, with telephone calls...

trouble: problem ☐ **I'm inclined:** I've a tendency ☐ **a teeny weeny bit:** a little bit ☐ **choosy and particular:** careful in choosing; particular, hard to satisfy; particular about food

on the off chance: in view of the possibility, in case

come along: appear, (fam.) show up, turn up

now and again: from time to time, now and then

right: as I want him to be, suitable

paused: stopped (for a short time) ☐ **stair-rail:** fixed bar as a protection against falling over

lips: he put the cigar between his lips ☐ **travelled...:** she examined him from head to foot ☐ **length:** long, length; wide, width; high, height; deep, depth ☐ **feet:** one foot, two feet

floor: horizontal division of a house ☐ **landing:** platform at the top of each set of stairs

flight (of stairs): set of stairs between two landings

yours," she said. "Here's your room. I do hope you'll like it." She took him into a small but charming front bedroom, switching on the light as she went in.

"The morning sun comes right in the window, Mr. Perkins. It *is* Mr. Perkins, isn't it?"

"No," he said. "It's Weaver."

"Mr. Weaver. How nice! I've put a water-bottle between the sheets to air them out, Mr. Weaver. It's such a comfort to have a hot water-bottle in a strange bed with
10 clean sheets, don't you agree? And you may light the gas fire at any time if you feel chilly."

"Thank you," Billy said. "Thank you ever so much." He noticed that the bedspread had been taken off the bed, and that the bedclothes had been neatly turned back on one side, all ready for someone to get in.

"I'm so glad you appeared," she said, looking earnestly into his face. "I was beginning to get worried."

"That's all right," Billy answered brightly. "You
20 mustn't worry about me." He put his suitcase on the chair and started to open it.

"And what about supper, my dear? Did you manage to get anything to eat before you came here?"

"I'm not a bit hungry, thank you," he said. "I think I'll just go to bed as soon as possible because tomorrow I've got to get up rather early and report to the office."

"Very well, then. I'll leave you now so that you can unpack. But before you go to bed, would you be kind enough to pop into the sitting-room on the ground floor
30 and sign the book? Everyone has to do that because it's the law of the land, and we don't want to go breaking any laws at *this* stage of the proceedings, do we?" She gave

do hope: (emphatic) I reallly hope, I honestly hope
took him into: take (sb.) to; I'll take you to town centre
switching on the light: ≠ switching off (the electricity)
right: directly, straight

weaver: (as a noun) one who weaves; weave, wove, woven, *tisser*
how nice: what a nice name! □ a **hot water-bottle** keeps you warm in
bed □ **sheet(s):** piece of cloth for bed □ **air out:** make (them) dry
and fresh □ **strange:** unfamiliar, not known
clean: ≠ dirty □ **agree:** have the same opinion □ **light the gas fire:**
put on the gas fire □ **chilly:** rather cold
thank you ever so much: thank you very much indeed
bedspread: ornamental covering spread over a bed
neatly: impeccably, carefully; neat, in good order

glad: happy, pleased □ **earnestly:** seriously; earnest, serious
to get worried: to worry, to feel anxiety
brightly: gaily, cheerfully; bright, cheerful and happy; bright faces
(lit up with joy); a bright smile
started to open it: or started opening it
what about: (suggesting) would you like?... □ **did you manage to...:**
were you able to...; can you manage to come tomorrow?
I'm not... hungry: be hungry; be thirsty; die of hunger; die of thirst
in the desert (for want of (sth.) to drink)
rather early: fairly early, pretty early; early ≠ late

unpack: take things out of suitcase □ **kind enough:** good enough
pop: come just for a minute □ **ground floor:** floor level with the
street (called "first floor" in the USA!)
law: rule, regulation □ **go breaking:** begin to disobey...
at this stage: at this point □ **proceeding(s):** course of action

him a little wave of the hand and went quickly out of the room and closed the door.

Now, the fact that his landlady appeared to be slightly off her rocker didn't worry Billy in the least. After all, she was not only harmless —there was no question about that— but she was also quite obviously a kind and generous soul. He guessed that she had probably lost a son in the war, or something like that, and had never got over it.

So a few minutes later, after unpacking his suitcase and
10 washing his hands, he trotted downstairs to the ground floor and entered the living-room. His landlady wasn't there, but the fire was glowing in the hearth, and the little dachshund was still sleeping in front of it. The room was wonderfully warm and cosy. I'm a lucky fellow, he thought, rubbing his hands. This is a bit of all right.

He found the guest-book lying open on the piano, so he took out his pen and wrote down his name and address. There were only two other entries above his on the page, and, as one always does with guest-books, he started
20 to read them. One was a Christopher Mulholland from Cardiff. The other was Gregory W. Temple from Bristol.

That's funny, he thought suddenly. Christopher Mulholland. It rings a bell.

Now where on earth had he heard that rather unusual name before?

Was he a boy at school? No. Was it one of his sister's numerous young men, perhaps, or a friend of his father's? No, no, it wasn't any of those. He glanced down again at the book.

30 *Christopher Mulholland   231 Cathedral Road, Cardiff*
Gregory W. Temple   27 Sycamore Drive, Bristol
As a matter of fact, now he came to think of it, he wasn't

wave: movement of the hand (to say (sb.) goodbye...); to wave (sb.) farewell □ **closed:** shut

now: (to call attention) now then, but □ **slightly off her rocker:** a little mad □ **...in the least:** didn't worry Billy at all

harmless: ≠ dangerous, harmful □ **question:** doubt

obviously: evidently, clearly □ **soul:** human being, person

guessed: supposed □ **son:** male child □ **war:** ≠ peace

had never got over it: had never been well and happy since the death of her son (so Billy imagines, but it is only guesswork: "he guessed"...)

entered the living-room: no preposition!

glowing: shining, burning without flame

was still sleeping: went on sleeping

cosy: comfortable □ **lucky:** having good fortune, luck

rubbing his hands (as a sign of happiness) □ **a bit...:** super

guest: person staying in a boarding-house, at a hotel...

pen: fountain pen, ball-point pen (to write with)

entries: (here) names; entry, item in a list

as one always does: as people always do in such a case

a Christopher Mulholland: a certain **Christopher Mulholland**

funny: strange □ **he thought:** he thought to himself

it rings a bell: it brings back vague memories

now: but □ **...on earth:** emphatic for "where?..." □ **unusual:** not common, rare ≠ usual □ **name:** first name or Christian name (Christopher); second name, family name, surname (Mulholland)

young men (who courted his sister), boyfriends, suitors

of his father's (friends) □ **glanced at:** took a quick look at; a glance, a quick look; at a glance, immediately on looking

road: (here) street (in a town or city)

drive: private road to house (through garden or park)

as a matter of fact...: in fact now that he was thinking of it

47

at all sure that the second name didn't have almost as much of a familiar ring about it as the first.

"Gregory Temple?" he said aloud, searching his memory. "Christopher Mulholland?..."

"Such charming boys," a voice behind him answered, and he turned and saw his landlady sailing into the room with a large silver tea-tray in her hands. She was holding it well out in front of her, and rather high up, as though the tray were a pair of reins on a frisky horse.

10 "They sound somehow familiar," he said.

"They do? How interesting!"

"I'm almost positive I've heard those names before somewhere. Isn't that queer? Maybe it was in the newspapers. They weren't famous in any way, were they? I mean famous cricketers or footballers or something like that?"

"Famous," she said, setting the tea-tray down on the low table in front of the sofa. "Oh no, I don't think they were famous. But they were extraordinarily handsome, both of 20 them, I can promise you that. They were tall and young and handsome, my dear, just exactly like you."

Once more, Billy glanced down at the book. "Look here," he said, noticing the dates. "This last entry is over two years old."

"It is?"

"Yes, indeed. And Christopher Mulholland's is nearly a year before that —more than *three years* ago."

"Dear me!" she said, shaking her head and heaving a dainty little sigh. "I would never have thought it. How 30 time does fly away from us all, doesn't it, Mr. Wilkins?"

"It's Weaver," Billy said. "W-e-a-v-e-r."

"Oh, of course it is!" she cried, sitting down on the

almost: nearly, practically

familiar ring: ...seemed or sounded as familiar to him

aloud: in a voice loud enough to be heard □ **searching his memory:** trying hard to find the name in his memory

such: he was such a charming fellow! (see position of "a")

sailing: walking with energy and confidence, triumphantly

silver: white precious metal □ **tray** with cups, teapot... on it □

well out: ≠ near, close □ **as though:** as if □ **were:** more literary than "was" □ **frisky:** full of life

somehow: in some way, for some reason

how interesting: how interesting this is!

positive: quite certain, sure; positively, certainly

queer: strange, odd □ **maybe:** perhaps

newspapers, papers like *The Times* □ **famous in any way:** wellknown in any domain or field of activity

setting: putting; set, set, set □ **low table:** coffee table, occasional table

handsome: (especially of men): good-looking

I can promise you that: you can be sure of it, I can assure you

once: once, twice, three times...; once more, once again

noticing: paying attention to □ **last:** ≠ first □ **over:** more than ≠ under, less than

yes, indeed: yes, it really is □ **Christopher Mulholland's** = Christopher Mulholland's entry (name and address)

dear me!: oh dear! □ **shaking her head and heaving a dainty sigh:** moving her head from side to side; heaving a sigh, *poussant un soupir*; dainty, small, delicate □ **fly:** pass quickly; time flies! (emphatic) how time does fly

of course: naturally! □ **she cried:** she said in a loud voice

sofa. "How silly of me. I do apologize. In one ear and out the other, that's me, Mr. Weaver."

"You know something?" Billy said. "Something that's really quite extraordinary about all this?"

"No, dear, I don't."

"Well, you see —both of these names, Mulholland and Temple, I not only seem to remember each one of them separately, so to speak, but somehow or other, in some peculiar way, they both appear to be sort of connected together as well. As though they were both famous for the same sort of thing, if you see what I mean —like... well... like Dempsey and Tunney, for example, or Churchill and Roosevelt."

"How amusing," she said, "but come over here now, dear, and sit down beside me on the sofa and I'll give you a nice cup of tea and a ginger biscuit before you go to bed."

"You really shouldn't bother," Billy said. "I didn't mean you to do anything like that." He stood by the piano, watching her as she fussed about with the cups and saucers. He noticed that she had small, white, quickly moving hands, and red finger-nails.

"I'm almost positive it was in the newspapers I saw them," Billy said. "I'll think of it in a second. I'm sure I will."

There is nothing more tantalizing than a thing like this which lingers just outside the borders of one's memory. He hated to give up.

"Now wait a minute," he said. "Wait just a minute. Mulholland... Christopher Mulholland... wasn't *that* the name of the Eton schoolboy who was on a walking-tour through the West Country, and then all of a sudden..."

"Milk?" she said. "And sugar?"

silly: stupid □ **I do apologize:** I'm really sorry □ **in one ear and out
the other:** what I hear goes in at one ear and out at the other, it has
no effect, it makes no impression on me
about all this: in all this

both of these names... appear: both these names appear, both appear,
they both appear, both of them appear
so to speak: if I may use this expression, as it were
peculiar: strange □ **sort of connected together:** in some way or degree
associated with each other □ **as well:** also, too
the same sort of thing: the same kind of thing
Dempsey...: famous boxers □ **for example:** (not e!) for instance

over here: over, from one side to the other; he has seen me, he is
coming over □ **beside:** near, close to
ginger: plant with strong taste used in cooking (*gingembre*)
bother (to do all that for me, it's too much work) □ **mean:** want,
expect, anticipate □ **by:** near
fussed about: kept herself busy in a nervous way
saucer(s): small dish on which a cup stands; flying saucer
moving: changing position □ **finger-nail(s):** hard flat piece at the end
of the finger; there are five fingers on each hand
I'll think of it: (here) I'll remember it; I can't think of it, I can't
remember it (notice "of")
tantalizing: tormenting, irritating, provoking
lingers: stays long □ **outside...:** at the limits of your...
hated: disliked, could not bear □ **give up:** abandon (give up finding
out who Mulholland and Temple were)

Eton: a famous English Public School □ **on a walking-tour:** note "on"
the West Country: the West of England □ **all of a sudden:** suddenly

"Yes, please. And then all of a sudden..."

"Eton schoolboy?" she said. "Oh no, my dear, that can't possibly be right because *my* Mr. Mulholland was certainly not an Eton schoolboy when he came to me. He was a Cambridge undergraduate. Come over here now and sit next to me and warm yourself in front of this lovely fire. Come on. Your tea's all ready for you." She patted the empty place beside her on the sofa, and she sat there smiling at Billy and waiting for him to come over.

10 He crossed the room slowly, and sat down on the edge of the sofa. She placed his teacup on the table in front of him.

"*There* we are," she said. "How nice and cosy this is, isn't it?"

Billy started sipping his tea. She did the same. For half a minute or so, neither of them spoke. But Billy knew that she was looking at him. Her body was half-turned towards him, and he could feel her eyes resting on his face, watching him over the rim of her teacup. Now and again,
20 he caught a whiff of a peculiar smell that seemed to emanate directly from her person. It was not in the least unpleasant, and it reminded him —well, he wasn't quite sure what it reminded him of. Pickled walnuts? New leather? Or was it the corridors of a hospital?

"Mr. Mulholland was a great one for his tea," she said at length. "Never in my life have I seen anyone drink as much tea as dear, sweet Mr. Mulholland."

"I suppose he left fairly recently." Billy said. He was still puzzling his head about the two names. He was
30 positive now that he had seen them in the newspapers —in the headlines.

"Left?" she said, arching her brows. "But my dear boy,

52

Yes please: yes, I'll have some (milk and sugar)

that can't possibly be right: it is certainly not the case; I cannot possibly come (absolutely not); right, correct, true
undergraduate: student who has not yet taken his first degree
next to: near □ **warm yourself:** get warm □ **lovely:** beautiful
come on: (encouragingly) come (don't be afraid)
patted: hit gently several times □ **empty:** (seat...) vacant
smiling at... waiting for: note the prepositions!
crossed: walked across, stepped across □ **edge:** outer limit
placed: put, set □ **in front of:** front ≠ back

there we are: now we are ready for tea

sipping: drinking a very small quantity at a time
neither of them spoke: none of them spoke, both kept silent

towards him: in his direction □ **resting on:** directed on, falling on
watching: looking carefully □ **rim:** edge, brim
caught: got, noticed for a moment □ **whiff:** *bouffée* □ **smell:** the smell of perfume... □ **not in the least:** not at all
unpleasant: ≠ pleasant □ **reminded him of:** made him think of
pickled: preserved in vinegar or salt water □ **walnut(s):** *noix*
leather: animal skin used for making shoes
was a great one for his tea: was very fond of tea
at length: after a long time, at (long) last □ **never in my life have I seen:** (emphatic) I have never seen □ **sweet:** lovable, pleasant, gentle or attractive in manner □ **fairly:** quite
puzzling his head: making a great effort to remember...

headlines are written in large letters above the articles
arching her (eye) brows (in surprise): brow: hair above eye

he never left. He's still here. Mr. Temple is also here. They're on the third floor, both of them together."

Billy set down his cup slowly on the table, and stared at his landlady. She smiled back at him, and then she put out one of her white hands and patted him comfortingly on the knee. "How old are you, my dear?" she asked.

"Seventeen."

"Seventeen!" she cried. "Oh, it's the perfect age! Mr. Mulholland was also seventeen. But I think he was a trifle
10 shorter than you are, in fact I'm sure he was, and his teeth weren't *quite* so white. You have the most beautiful teeth, Mr. Weaver, did you know that?"

"They're not as good as they look," Billy said. "They've got simply masses of fillings in them at the back."

"Mr. Temple, of course, was a little older," she said, ignoring his remark. "He was actually twenty-eight. And yet I never would have guessed it if he hadn't told me, never in my whole life. There wasn't a *blemish* on
20 his body."

"A what?" Billy said.

"His skin was *just* like a baby's."

There was a pause. Billy picked up his teacup and took another sip of his tea, then he set it down again gently in its saucer. He waited for her to say something else, but she seemed to have lapsed into another of her silences. He sat there staring straight ahead of him into the far corner of the room, biting his lower lip.

"That parrot," he said at last. "You know something?
30 It had me completely fooled when I first saw it through the window from the street. I could have sworn it was alive."

"Alas, no longer."

54

left: leave, left, left; "Bye", he said on leaving (on!)

on the third floor: on!; floor, storey, (Am.) story

stared at: looked fixedly at... with wide open eyes

smiled back: smiled in her turn (at, not to!) □ **put out:** held out her hand towards him □ **comfortingly:** as if to give him comfort or sympathy □ **knee:** he was on his knees looking for (sth.) under his bed

the perfect age: what for?... (read on!)

a trifle: a little, somewhat; a trifle too long

shorter: smaller □ **teeth:** a dentist treats your teeth; thirty-two teeth (one tooth!)

as they look: as they seem; he looks young for his age

simply: in simple terms, in actual fact □ **masses of fillings:** masses (fam.) lots of; filling(s), metal with which a bad tooth is filled in by a dentist; fill *with;* full *of*

ignoring: refusing to take notice of □ **actually:** in fact

guessed: known by guessing, on supposition

never in my whole life: (emphatic) never ever □ **blemish:** mark that spoilt the beauty or perfection of his body, imperfection, defect, flaw (physical or moral)

skin: your skin turns brown in the sun □ **baby's** (skin)

a pause: a silence □ **picked up:** took hold of and lifted

sip: very small quantity at a time □ **gently:** ≠ violently, roughly

something else (in addition, another thing)

lapsed: fallen gradually; lapse into silence, into bad habits...

straight ahead of: directly, right in front of □ **the far corner:** the most distant corner □ **biting his lower lip:** bite, bit, bitten, cut with the teeth; lower lip ≠ upper lip

fooled: duped, deceived (I really thought it was living)

sworn: (fam.) said firmly, solemnly □ **alive:** living ≠ dead

alas, no longer: alas, it is no longer alive

"It's most terribly clever the way it's been done," he said. "It doesn't look in the least bit dead. Who did it?"

"I did."

"*You* did?"

"Of course,"she said. "And you have met my little Basil as well?" She nodded towards the dachshund curled up so comfortably in front of the fire. Billy looked at it. And suddenly, he realized that this animal had all the time been just as silent and motionless as the parrot. He
10 put out a hand and touched it gently on the top of its back. The back was hard and cold, and when he pushed the hair to one side with his fingers, he could see the skin underneath, greyish-black and dry and perfectly preserved.

"Good gracious me," he said. "How absolutely fascinating." He turned away from the dog and stared with deep admiration at the little woman beside him on the sofa. "It must be most awfully difficult to do a thing like that."

"Not in the least," she said. "I stuff *all* my little pets
20 myself when they pass away. Will you have another cup of tea?"

"No, thank you," Billy said. The tea tasted faintly of bitter almonds, and he didn't much care for it.

"You did sign the book, didn't you?"

"Oh, yes."

"That's good. Because later on, if I happen to forget what you were called, then I can always come down here and look it up. I still do that almost every day with Mr. Mulholland and Mr... Mr..."

30 "Temple," Billy said. "Gregory Temple. Excuse my asking, but haven't there been *any* other guests here except them in the last two or three years?"

56

clever: adroit, skilful; clever with one's hands □ **way:** manner, method (the way (in which) it has been done is very clever indeed)

you **did:** italics are often used in English for emphasis
met: (amusingly here) been introduced to
nodded: inclined her head □ **curled up:** huddled up, hunched up (p. 36, l. 18)
realized: understood, was fully conscious
motionless: without any movement, quite still
top: the highest part (≠ bottom)
back: upper surface of animal's body □ **hard:** firm ≠ soft

underneath: under the hair □ **greyish:** more or less grey
good gracious me: (in admiration or surprise): dear me! oh dear! Heavens above! □ **he turned:** no reflexive pronoun!

awfully: (fam.) very

stuff: fill carcass of animal for preservation □ **pet(s):** animal kept as a companion □ **pass away:** come to the end of life, die, pass on, pass over
tasted of: *avait un goût* (taste) *de* □ **faintly:** a little
bitter: ≠ sweet □ **almond(s):** *amande* □ **care for:** like (sth. or sb.); I don't care for tea, I like coffee better; I don't care much for him, I prefer his brother
later on: in the future □ **if I happen to...:** in case I forget, if it so happens □ **what you were called:** what your name was
look it up: look up, find (information) in a (reference) book...; look up a word in a dictionary only if the context doesn't help!

my asking: the fact that I am asking (verbal noun!)
the last two or three years: note the position of "last"

57

Holding her teacup high in one hand, inclining her head slightly to the left, she looked up at him out of the corners of her eyes and gave him another gentle little smile.

"No, my dear," she said.   "Only you."

high: ≠ low □ **in one hand** (not two! one ≠ a) □ **inclining her head to the left:** nodding to the left (p. 56, l. 6)

gave him another smile: give (sb.) a smile, smile at (sb.) (note the preposition "at", but one says "smile to oneself")

Grammaire au fil des nouvelles

Traduisez les phrases suivantes inspirées du texte (le premier chiffre renvoie aux pages, les suivants aux lignes) :

Il se pourrait qu'ils vous prennent (34.11).

Présentez-vous au directeur d'agence dès que vous vous serez installé (**when, while, as soon as** + ... 34.19).

Il s'arrêta de marcher (**stop, start, go on** + ... 36.12).

Il y aurait des tas de gens à qui parler (suppression du relatif et rejet de la préposition, 36.29,30).

Les œufs sont chers en ce moment (emploi de **the**, 40.25).

Entrez, je vous prie (forme d'insistance, 40.29).

Vous pouvez allumer le chauffage à *n'importe quel* moment (44.11).

Nous ne voulons pas enfreindre la loi, *n'est-ce pas ?* (**want** + ... 44.31).

Ils étaient très élégants tous les deux (**both**, 48.19).

Vous ne devriez pas vous tracasser (auxiliaire modal, 50.17).

Comme tout ceci est agréable et douillet ! (**how** exclamatif, 52.13).

Pendant une demi-minute aucun des deux ne parla (place de **a, an ; neither** ; une seule négation ! 52.16).

Jamais je n'ai vu personne boire *autant* de thé (structure avec **never** en tête de phrase ; verbes de perception, 52.26).

Il attendit qu'elle dît quelque chose d'*autre* (proposition infinitive introduite par **for** avec **wait**, 54.25).

Il se mordait *la* lèvre inférieure (emploi du possessif devant noms de parties du corps ; emploi du comparatif, s'agissant de deux, 54.28).

J'aurais pu jurer qu'il était vivant (54.31).

Vous avez bien signé le livre, *n'est-ce pas ?* (forme d'insistance, 56.24).

Excusez-moi de le demander, mais *n'y a-t-il pas eu* d'autres pensionnaires au cours des deux ou trois dernières années ? (gérondif avec adjectif possessif ; place de **last, first**, 56.30,31,32).

I SPY[1]

by Graham Greene (1904-1991)

Graham Greene was born in 1904 and educated first at Berkhamsted where his father was headmaster and later at Balliol College, Oxford. In 1926 he was converted to Catholicism. This deeply coloured his fiction.

In 1928 he published *Brighton Rock* in which his religious preoccupations came to the foreground. It was fully expressed in *The Power and the Glory* which came out in 1940. Other wellknown works include *The Heart of the Matter* (1948), *The Quiet American* (1955), *Travels with my Aunt* (1969)... In all, Graham Greene, who has travelled extensively as a journalist throughout the world, has published some thirty novels, "entertainments" like *The Third Man,* Travel Books, plays, short stories (*Collected Short Stories,* Bodley Head and Heinemann publishers; *Twenty-One Stories,* Penguin Books Limited).

There is often a detective side to Graham Greene's novels. They remind you of thrillers but together with the suspense there are deep psychological, moral or metaphysical implications. In this respect, *I Spy* in its modest way is a good example of that interesting combination.

(1) "I spy (watch) with my little eye sth. beginning with..." (child game); **spy:** watch (sb.) when he doesn't know he's being watched; **a spy:** (sb.) who gives information to an enemy.

Charlie Stowe waited until he heard his mother snore before he got out of bed. Even then he moved with caution and tiptoed to the window. The front of the house was irregular, so that it was possible to see a light burning in his mother's room. But now all the windows were dark. A searchlight passed across the sky, lighting the banks of cloud and probing the dark deep spaces between, seeking enemy airships. The wind blew from the sea, and Charlie Stowe could hear behind his mother's snores the
10 beating of the waves. A draught through the cracks in the window-frame stirred his night-shirt. Charlie Stowe was frightened.

But the thought of the tobacconist's shop which his father kept down a dozen wooden stairs drew him on. He was twelve years old, and already boys at the County School mocked him because he had never smoked a cigarette. The packets were piled twelve deep below, Gold Flake and Players, De Reszke, Abdulla, Woodbines, and the little shop lay under a thin haze of stale smoke which
20 would completely disguise his crime. That it was a crime to steal some of his father's stock Charlie Stowe had no doubt, but he did not love his father; his father was unreal to him, a wraith, pale, thin, indefinite, who noticed him only spasmodically and left even punishment to his mother. For his mother he felt a passionate demonstrative love; her large boisterous presence and her noisy charity filled the world for him; from her speech he judged her the friend of everyone, from the rector's wife to the "dear Queen", except the "Huns", the monsters who lurked in
30 Zeppelins in the clouds. But his father's affection and dislike were as indefinite as his movements. Tonight he had said he would be in Norwich, and yet you never

62

snore: make a noise with one's nose when sleeping; a snore
even: even a child knows that □ **moved:** changed position
caution: care □ **tiptoed:** walked on tiptoe *(pointe des pieds)*
a light burning: a lamp (switched) on; light: source of light (which makes things visible); light ≠ darkness; to light
searchlight: rotating light for detecting enemy presence
probing: exploring □ **deep:** large □ **space(s):** intervals
seeking: looking for □ **airship(s):** dirigible, balloon

wave(s): sea movement □ **draught... cracks:** current of air through the small openings □ **frame:** fixed part of window □ **stirred his night-shirt:** made his night-shirt move □ **frightened:** afraid
the thought of: the fact of thinking of
dozen: 12 □ **wooden:** wood *(bois)* □ **stair(s):** *marche* □ **drew him on:** encouraged him to go on □ **county:** division of G.B., shire, like Lancashire... □ **mocked him:** laughed at him
piled twelve deep below: in piles of twelve packets one below (under) the other □ **Gold Flake... are** names of cigarettes
thin: ≠ thick □ **haze:** thin cloud □ **stale:** ≠ fresh
disguise: hide, keep secret □ **crime:** any illegal action
steal: steal (sth. from sb.), rob (sb. of sth.)
unreal: non-existing, imaginary, illusory (≠ real)
wraith: spectre, spirit, ghost □ **noticed:** paid attention to
spasmodically: irregularly, occasionally, now and then

boisterous: exuberant, noisy, making too much noise
filled...: was his universe □ **from her speech...:** from what she said, he thought... □ **rector:** clergyman in charge of a parish
Huns: (pejorative) Germans □ **lurked:** were hidden (out of view), in wait or ready to attack □ **Zeppelin(s):** airship
dislike: likes and dislikes (what you like and don't like)
yet: however, still

knew. Charlie Stowe had no sense of safety as he crept down the wooden stairs. When they creaked he clenched his fingers on the collar of his night-shirt.

At the bottom of the stairs he came out quite suddenly into the little shop. It was too dark to see his way, and he did not dare touch the switch. For half a minute he sat in despair on the bottom step with his chin cupped in his hands. Then the regular movement of the searchlight was reflected through an upper window and the boy had time
10 to fix in memory the pile of cigarettes, the counter, and the small hole under it. The footsteps of a policeman on the pavement made him grab the first packet to his hand and dive for the hole. A light shone along the floor and a hand tried the door, then the footsteps passed on, and Charlie cowered in the darkness.

At last he got his courage back by telling himself in his curiously adult way that if he were caught now there was nothing to be done about it, and he might as well have his smoke. He put a cigarette in his mouth and then
20 remembered that he had no matches. For a while he dared not move. Three times the searchlight lit the shop, as he muttered taunts and encouragements. "May as well be hung for a sheep," "Cowardy, cowardy custard," grown-up and childish exhortations oddly mixed.

But as he moved he heard footfalls in the street, the sound of several men walking rapidly. Charlie Stowe was old enough to feel surprise that anybody was about. The footsteps came nearer, stopped; a key was turned in the shop door, a voice said: "Let him in," and then he heard
30 his father, "If you wouldn't mind being quiet, gentlemen. I don't want to wake up the family." There was a note unfamiliar to Charlie in the undecided voice. A torch

safety: security □ **crept:** moved slowly, secretly, cautiously
creaked: made a noise □ **clenched:** pressed firmly together
finger(s): there are five fingers on each hand
bottom: ≠ top □ **suddenly:** all of a sudden
to see his way: to see where he was going
dare: have the courage □ **the switch** (to switch on the electricity)
step: stair □ **chin:** part of face below mouth □ **cupped in his hands:**
placed in his hands in the shape (form) of a cup
upper window: ≠ lower window (top ≠ bottom)
counter: table in a shop at which people are served
hole: empty space (to hide in) □ **footstep(s):** sound made by foot
when walking □ **pavement:** (Am.) sidewalk □ **grab:** seize
dive: rush □ **shone:** looked bright □ **floor:** surface of a room on
which one walks □ **tried** (to open) **the door** to see if it was shut
cowered: bent low (like a frightened dog)
at last: after a long time, in the end
adult: grown-up (l. 23) □ **caught** (stealing): discovered

smoke: (fam.) I'll have a smoke (a cigarette)
matches (to light his cigarette with) □ **a while:** a short time
lit: light, lit or lighted, lit or lighted
muttered taunts: murmured sarcasms □ **may...:** *autant être pendu*
à voler un mouton (qu'un agneau) □ **cowardy custard:** a coward ≠
a brave person with energy; custard, *crème (molle)* □ **oddly:**
strangely □ **footfall(s):** sound made by foot when walking, footstep
(l. 11) □ **several:** three, or more
about: there, in the area, (Am.) around
key: do you have a key to this door? (to open or shut...)
let him in: ≠ let him out (let him go in...)
mind + ing: object to + ing □ **quiet:** silent, calm
wake up: cause to stop sleeping
unfamiliar to: unknown to □ **torch:** electric hand-light

flashed and the electric globe burst into blue light. The boy held his breath; he wondered whether his father would hear his heart beating, and he clutched his night-shirt tightly and prayed, "O God, don't let me be caught." Through a crack in the counter he could see his father where he stood, one hand held to his high stiff collar, between two men in bowler hats and belted mackintoshes. They were strangers.

"Have a cigarette," his father said in a voice dry as a
10 biscuit. One of the men shook his head. "It wouldn't do, not when we are on duty. Thank you all the same." He spoke gently, but without kindness: Charlie Stowe thought his father must be ill.

"Mind if I put a few in my pocket?" Mr. Stowe asked, and when the man nodded he lifted a pile of Gold Flake and Players from a shelf and caressed the packets with the tips of his fingers.

"Well," he said, "there's nothing to be done about it, and I may as well have my smokes." For a moment
20 Charlie Stowe feared discovery, his father stared round the shop so thoroughly; he might have been seeing it for the first time. "It's a good little business," he said, "for those that like it. The wife will sell out, I suppose. Else the neighbours'll be wrecking it. Well, you want to be off. A stitch in time. I'll get my coat."

"One of us'll come with you, if you don't mind," said the stranger gently.

"You needn't trouble. It's on the peg here. There, I'm
30 all ready."

The other man said in an embarrassed way, "Don't you want to speak to your wife?" The thin voice was decided,

66

flashed...: shone suddenly and the blue light of the globe appeared abruptly ☐ **breath:** respiration ☐ **wondered...:** asked himself if **clutched:** seized, grabbed ☐ **tightly:** firmly
prayed: talked to God, asking him a favour; say a prayer

stiff: rigid, not flexible ☐ **collar:** shirt collar
bowler hat(s): *chapeau melon* ☐ **belted mackintoshes:** raincoats with belts *(ceintures)* ☐ **strangers:** people he didn't know
dry: (here) cold, without warmness or feeling
shook his head (to say "no") ☐ **do:** be right (professionally)
on duty: working ☐ **all the same:** in spite of that, nevertheless
gently: quietly, slowly ☐ **kindness:** sympathy, love for others, benevolence; kind, kind-hearted ☐ **ill:** sick, in bad health
mind: do you mind if..., have you any objection to my putting...
nodded: (to say "yes" with his head) ☐ **lifted:** took, picked up
shelf (fixed to wall for putting things on) ☐ **tip(s):** pointed or thin end of (sth.); fingertip; have something at the tip of one's tongue, be about to remember (a name...)

feared...: was afraid of being discovered ☐ **stared:** looked fixedly ☐ **thoroughly:** carefully ☐ **he might...:** one would have thought he was seeing it... ☐ **business:** money-earning activity
sell out: sell all the stock
else: if not ☐ **neighbours:** people living near ☐ **wreck:** destroy
be off: go ☐ **a stitch in time (saves nine):** (proverb) a piece of work done now saves a lot of time later; stitch, point *(tricot...)*; save time; save money

you needn't trouble (to come, don't worry) ☐ **peg:** piece of metal... fixed to a wall for hanging coats and hats on
embarrassed: feel embarrassed, uneasy, ill at ease
wife: they are husband and wife (they are married)

"Not me. Never do today what you can put off till tomorrow. She'll have her chance later, won't she?"

"Yes, yes," one of the strangers said and he became very cheerful and encouraging. "Don't you worry too much. While there's life..." and suddenly his father tried to laugh.

When the door had closed Charlie Stowe tiptoed upstairs and got into bed. He wondered why his father had left the house again so late at night and who the strangers
10 were. Surprise and awe kept him for a little while awake. It was as if a familiar photograph had stepped from the frame to reproach him with neglect. He remembered how his father had held tight to his collar and fortified himself with proverbs, and he thought for the first time that, while his mother was boisterous and kindly his father was very like himself, doing things in the dark which frightened him. It would have pleased him to go down to his father and tell him that he loved him, but he could hear through the window the quick steps going away. He was
20 alone in the house with his mother, and he fell asleep.

not me: certainly not □ **never put off till tomorrow what you can do today** (Mr. Stowe is nervous) □ **chance:** occasion, opportunity
became: become, became, become; get + adjective
cheerful: bringing happiness □ **don't you worry:** (emphatic) don't worry (be anxious) □ **while there is life** (there is hope)
...laugh: made an effort to laugh to "cheer" himself up
closed: was shut □ **tiptoed...:** went upstairs on tiptoe (p. 62, l. 3)

awe: respect mixed with fear (p. 66, l. 20)
awake: not sleeping □ **stepped from:** walked out of
frame: border of wood... for a photo □ **neglect:** ≠ attention, care, affection □ **held tight:** held tightly, firmly (p. 66, l. 3)
proverbs like "May as well be hung for a sheep as for a lamb"
while: (implying a contrast) whereas □ **kindly:** friendly
in the dark: in secret
frightened...: made him afraid □ **it would have pleased him to...:** he would have liked to...; do as you please, do as you like

alone: by himself, with nobody else □ **fell asleep:** fall asleep, go to sleep; go back to sleep

Grammaire au fil des nouvelles

Traduisez les phrases suivantes inspirées du texte (le premier chiffre renvoie aux pages, les suivants aux lignes) :

Charlie Stowe attendit jusqu'au moment où il entendit ronfler sa mère... Il était possible de voir brûler une lampe (verbes de perception +..., 62.1,4).

Penser au bureau de tabac *que* tenait son père une *douzaine de* marches plus bas le poussait à continuer (62.13).

Ce soir il avait dit qu'il serait à Norwich et pourtant *on* ne savait jamais (style indirect, 62.32).

Il n'osa pas toucher l'interrupteur... Vous n'avez pas besoin de vous inquiéter (**dare** et **need**, 64.6 et 66.29).

Il retrouva son courage *en se disant* que s'il *était* pris il n'y aurait rien à y faire (subjonctif prétérit, 64.16).

Si ça ne vous dérangeait pas de ne pas faire de bruit. Je ne veux pas réveiller la famille (verbes + gérondif, 64.30 ; **want** +..., 64.31).

Il saisit fermement sa chemise de nuit (place de l'adverbe, 66.3).

Mon Dieu, faites que je ne sois pas pris (impératif négatif et **let**, 66.4).

L'un des hommes secoua *la* tête (noms de parties du corps précédés de..., 66.10).

Charlie Stowe pensa que son père devait être malade (quasi-certitude, 66.12).

C'est un bon petit commerce pour *ceux qui* aiment ça (66.22,23).

Vous ne voulez pas parler à votre femme ? (forme interro-négative, 66.31,32).

Elle aura sa chance plus tard, *n'est-ce pas* ? (68.2).

Ne vous inquiétez donc pas trop (impératif négatif avec insistance ; "trop" modifiant un verbe, 68.4).

Il se demanda qui étaient les inconnus (style indirect, 68.8).

Les bruits de pas d'un agent de police l'amenèrent à saisir le premier paquet qui était à sa portée (**make** et **let** +... 64.12).

DEAR ALEXANDROS

by John Updike (born in 1932)

John Updike was born in Pennsylvania and educated at Harvard and the Ruskin School of Drawing and fine Art at Oxford. From 1955 to 1957 he wrote for *The New Yorker*, contributing short stories, essays and poems. He has published many books, among them novels *(Rabbit Run, The Centaur, Couples...)* and collections of short stories : *Pigeon Feathers and Other Stories, The Music School, Bech: A Book.*

According to John Updike himself his subject is "the American Protestant small town middle-class" whose supposedly respectable façade he describes with great irony like in *Dear Alexandros* taken from *Pigeon Feathers and Other Stories* available in Penguin Books. His prose is polished and precise. He is a remarkable stylist.

Translation of a letter written by Alexandros Koundouriotis, Needy Child No. 26,511 in the records of Hope, Incorporated, an international charity with headquarters in New York.

July 1959

Dear Mr. and Mrs. Bentley:

Dear American Parents, first of all I want to inquire about your good health, and then, if you ask me, tell you that I am keeping well, for which I thank God, and hope
10 that it is the same with you. May God keep you always well, and grant you every happiness and joy. With great eagerness I was looking forward again this month to receiving a letter from you, but unfortunately I have again not received one. So I am worried about you, for I am longing to hear about you, dear American Parents. You show such a great interest in me, and every month I receive your help. Over here it is very hot at this time of the year, for we are in the heart of the summer. The work out in the fields is very tiring, as I hear the older people
20 saying. As for me, when I have no work at home I go down to the sea for a swim, and enjoy the sea with my friends. For at this time of the year the sea is lovely. So much for my news. Vacations continue, until it is time for the schools to reopen, when with new strength and joy we shall begin our lessons again. Today that I am writing to you I received again the $8.00 that you sent me, for the month of July, and I thank you very much. With this money I shall buy whatever I need, and we shall also buy some flour for our bread. In closing, I send you greetings
30 from my granny and my sister, and hope that my letter finds you in good health and joy. I shall be looking forward to receiving a letter from you, to hear about you and how you

72

translation: translate from French into English
needy: poor □ **record(s):** *dossier* □ **hope:** *espoir* □ **Incorporated:** *constitué en société* □ **...charity with headquarters:** charity, organisation that gives help to the poor; headquarters, place, office from which operations are controlled; head office

inquire: ask for information; inquiry office
health: smoking damages your health
I am keeping well: I am well, in good health (≠ unwell)
may God...: I hope God keeps you always well
grant you: give you
eagerness: enthusiasm □ **I was looking forward... to receiving:** look forward to + ing, anticipate, expect with pleasure
worried: anxious, concerned □ **for:** because
longing: strongly desiring □ **hear about:** receive news from

help: (financial) aid □ **this time of the year:** this season
the heart of the summer: the middle of the summer
field(s): cultivated land □ **tiring:** causing fatigue
as for me: I personally, as far as I am concerned
go... for a swim: swim (like a fish in water) □ **enjoy:** get pleasure from; I enjoy music, I like music
so much for...: enough about me □ **vacation(s)** (Am.): holiday; on vacation, on holiday (no s!) □ **strength:** energy; strong ≠ weak

$: dollar; $ 1 = 100 cents □ **sent:** send, sent, sent
July: July is the seventh month of the year
whatever I need: everything I need, all I want
flour is white □ **in closing I send you greetings:** on finishing my letter I send you good wishes □ **granny:** (fam.) grandmother; grandad, (fam.) grandfather
letter: letterbox, pillarbox, (Am.) mailbox

are spending your summer. I greet you with much affection.

                                                    Your son,
                                                    Alexandros.

Reply from Kenneth Bentley, American Parent No. 10,638.

10   25 September
Dear Alexandros:
We are all sorry that you should worry about us because you have not received a letter from us. I fear we are not regular in writing as you are, but the pretentiously named organization which delivers our letters seems to be very slow, they take about three months as far as I can tell. Perhaps they send them by way of China.

You describe the Greek summer very beautifully. It is autumn now in New York City. The sad little trees along
20 the somewhat sad little street where I live now are turning yellow, the ones that are not already dead. The pretty girls that walk along the main streets are putting on hats again. In New York the main streets run north and south so that there is usually a sunny side and a shady side and now people cross the street to be on the sunny side because the sun is no longer too warm. The sky is very blue and some evenings, after I eat in a luncheonette or restaurant, I walk a few blocks over to the East River to watch the boats and look at Brooklyn, which is another section of the
30 immense city.

Mrs. Bentley and I no longer live together. I had not intended to tell you this but now the sentence is typed and

74

greet: say hello to, (in a letter) write words expressing respect, friendship...

son: she has two children, one son, John, and one daughter, Mary

reply: answer; to reply, to answer

25 September: read September the twenty fifth or the twenty fifth of September

worry about (over): be anxious, uneasy, troubled

I fear: I am afraid

named: called; name, give a name to

delivers: the postman delivers the letters every morning

slow: ≠ quick □ **about:** a little more or less □ **as far as I can tell:** as far as I know, *autant que je sache* □ **by way of China:** through China □ **Greek:** from Greece

autumn: fall (Am.) □ **sad:** miserable, unhappy; sadness ≠ joy

somewhat: rather, in some degree □ **turning yellow:** getting yellow, becoming yellow □ **the ones that:** those which

main: most important □ **putting on:** put on (clothes) ≠ take off

run north: notice the use of "run" here

usually: generally □ **sunny:** bright with sunshine □ **shady:** (≠ sunny) full of shade □ **people cross:** "people" is plural; these people are ridiculous; few people do that

luncheonette: lunch, luncheon, meal taken in the middle of the day

block(s) (Am.): the distance between two streets

immense: huge, mammoth

I had not intended to...: it was not my intention to

sentence: *phrase* □ **typed:** written with a type writer

I see no harm in it.   Perhaps already you were wondering why I am writing from New York City instead of from Greenwich.   Mrs. Bentley and little Amanda and Richard all still live in our nice home in Greenwich and the last time I saw them looked very well.   Amanda now is starting kindergarten and was very excited and will never wear dungarees or overalls any more but insists on wearing dresses because that is what makes little girls look nice, she thinks.   This makes her mother rather angry, especially on

10 Saturdays and Sundays when Amanda plays mostly in the dirt with the neighbour children.   Richard walks very well now and does not like his sister teasing him.   As who does?   I go to see them once a week and pick up my mail and your last letter was one of the letters I picked up and was delighted to read.   Mrs. Bentley asked me to answer it, which I was delighted to do, because she had written you the last time.   In fact I do not think she did, but writing letters was one thing she was not good at, although it was her idea for us to subscribe to Hope, Incorporated, and I

20 know she loves you very much, and was especially happy to learn that you plan to begin school with 'new strength and joy'.

There has been much excitement in the United States over the visit of the head of Soviet Russia, Mr. Khrushchev.   He is a very talkative and self-confident man and in meeting some of our own talkative and self-confident politicians there has been some friction, much of it right on television where everybody could see.   My main worry was that he would be shot but I don't think he will be shot any

30 more.   His being in the country has been a funny feeling, as if you have swallowed a penny, but the American people are so anxious for peace that they will put up with small

harm: damage, wrong; do harm ≠ do good □ **wondering:** asking yourself □ **instead of:** in place of; I had rather stay in bed instead of going to work!

still live: go on living □ **the last time:** ≠ the first time

looked very well: seemed to be in perfect health

kindergarten: school for children from four to six

dungarees, overalls are worn by babies, workers... over ordinary clothes to keep them clean

angry: be angry with (sb.), be angry at (sth.); he was angry, he was red in the face □ **mostly:** generally, most of the time

dirt: ≠ cleanness □ **neighbour children** live in houses nearby

teasing: mocking □ **as who does?:** who would? (like to be teased)

once a week: one time every week □ **I pick up my mail:** I get my mail (letters, postcards, parcels...)

delighted: very happy, very pleased; delight, great joy

last: ≠ first; last but one (that comes just before the last)

good at: he's good at French but he's bad at maths (at!)

subscribe to: become a member of; pay one's subscription; a subscriber; he subscribes liberally to charities

you plan to: you intend to; we plan to go camping next summer; make plans; what are your plans for the weekend?

excitement: strong emotion, agitation □ **over:** about

the head: the leader; headmaster; be at the head of

talkative: fond of talking □ **self-confident:** self-assured

politician(s): one engaged or interested in politics

right: directly, straight; live ≠ recorded

main: chief, principal □ **worry:** cause of anxiety, concern

shot: shot to death (by a gun, a pistol...)

funny: strange, peculiar □ **feeling:** impression

swallowed: absorbed □ **penny:** penny piece, penny coin

anxious for: strongly desiring □ **put up with:** bear

discomforts if there is any chance it will do any good.   The United States, as perhaps you will learn in school, was for many years an isolated country and there still is a perhaps childish wish that other nations, even though we are a great power, just let us alone, and then the sun will shine.

That was not a very good paragraph and perhaps the man or woman who kindly translates these letters for us will kindly omit it.   I have a cold in my chest that mixes with a great deal of cigarette smoke and makes me very confused,
10 especially after I have been sitting still for a while.

I am troubled because I imagine I hear you asking, ' Then were Mr. and Mrs. Bentley, who sent me such happy letters from America, and photographs of their children, and a sweater and a jackknife at Christmas, telling lies?   Why do they not live together any more? '   I do not wish you to worry.   Perhaps in your own village you have husbands and wives who quarrel.   Perhaps they quarrel but continue to live together but in America where we have so much plumbing and fast automobiles and rapid highways we have
20 forgotten how to live with inconveniences, although I admit that my present mode of life is something of an inconvenience to me.   Or perhaps in your schooling, if you keep at it, and I hope you will, the priests or nuns will have you read the very great Greek poem the *Iliad*, in which the poet Homer tells of Helen who left her husband to live with Paris among the Trojans.   It is something like that with the Bentleys, except that I, a man, have gone to live among the Trojans, leaving my wife at home.   I do not know if the *Iliad* is a part of your schooling, and would be curious to
30 know.   Your nation should be very proud of producing masterpieces which the whole world can enjoy.   In the

78

discomfort(s): difficulty, trouble, worry (≠ comfort)

the United States... was: "was", not "were"!

isolated: cut off from the rest of the world

childish: puerile □ **wish:** desire □ **even though:** even if

power: nation; the Great Powers □ **let us alone...:** abstain from interfering with us and then everything will be fine

who kindly translates: who is good enough to translate

cold in the chest: as opposed to a cold in the head

a great deal of: a lot of □ **confused:** lost, unable to think straight, muddled □ **still:** without moving □ **for a while:** for some time; a while, a period of time □ **troubled:** worried, preoccupied; be troubled about (sth.)

sweater: pullover □ **jackknife:** pocket knife □ **telling lies:** ≠ speaking the truth; a lie, an untruth; a liar is a man who lies or tells lies □ **husbands:** they are husband and wife, they are married

quarrel: fight, have a violent argument, have a quarrel; quarrelsome, fond of quarelling

plumbing: bathroom installations □ **highway(s):** (Am.) motorways... (in America where we have great material comfort)

my present mode of life: the way I live these days

schooling: education at school

keep at it: ≠ give up □ **priest(s):** clergyman □ **nun(s):** woman in the service of God □ **have you read:** make you read

among: in the middle of

the Bentleys: s! (Mr. and Mrs. Bentley); the Browns...

at home: come home, go home, return home... (no preposition!)

curious to know: interested to know; curiosity

proud: feeling satisfaction, proud of (one's success)

masterpiece: piece of art... which is the best of its type

United States the great writers produce works which people do not enjoy, because they are so depressing to read.

But we were not telling lies, Mrs. Bentley and Amanda and Richard and I were very happy and to a degree are yet. Please continue to send us your wonderful letters, they will go to Greenwich, and we will all enjoy them. We will continue to send you the money for which you say you are grateful, though the money we give you this way is not a fourth of the money we used to spend
10 for alcoholic drinks. Not that Mrs. Bentley and I drank all these alcoholic drinks. We had many friends who helped us, most of them very tedious people, although perhaps you would like them more than I do. Certainly they would like you more than they liked me.

I am so happy that you live near the sea where you can swim and relax from the tiring work of the fields. I was born far inland in America, a thousand miles from any ocean, and did not come to love the sea until I was grown
20 up and married. So in that sense you are luckier than I. Certainly to be near the sea is a great blessing, and I remember often thinking how nice it was that my own children should know what it was to run on the sand of the pretty though not large beach at Greenwich, and to have that great calm horizon over their shoulders.

Now I must end, for I have agreed to take a young woman out to dinner, a young woman who, you will be interested to hear, is herself Greek in origin, though born in America, and who has much of the beauty of your race. But I have
30 already cruelly burdened our translator. My best wishes to your granny, who has taken such good care of you since your mother died, and to your sister, whose welfare and

works: the complete works of Shakespeare
depressing: disheartening; depressed, disheartened, dejected, downcast

to a degree: to a certain degree, up to a certain extent
are yet: still are (happy), continue to be (happy)
we will all enjoy them: enjoy (sth.), like (sth.) (same meaning, same construction!)
grateful: thankful □ **(in) this way:** in this manner
fourth: one of four equal parts into which (sth.) is or could be divided; half, third, fourth, fifth...

most of them: the majority of them □ **tedious:** uninteresting, dull, boring; a tedious books makes you go to sleep; tediousness, tedium, boredom

near the sea: by the sea, by the seaside
relax: become less tense or active, rest, (fam.) unwind
inland: in the interior of a country, far from the sea
come to: begin to □ **until I was grown up:** before I became an adult (a grown-up) □ **luckier:** lucky, having luck, good fortune
blessing: (God's) favour, (sth.) that brings happiness
I remember...: I remember I often thought to myself...
sand: there is plenty of sand by the sea and in a desert
pretty: nice, lovely □ **though:** but, yet □ **beach:** (sand) beach, land next to the sea □ **shoulder(s):** part of body joining arm to trunk □ **end:** close (p. 72, 1. 29) □ **I have agreed to:** I have arranged to; agree with (sb.), share his opinion ≠ disagree
to hear: learn □ **though born:** though she was born

burdened: given too much work to; burden, (sth.) difficult to carry or bear □ **taken... care of:** looked after
welfare: comfort and happiness, well-being

good health is such a large concern in your heart.

Sincerely,

Kenneth Bentley.

PS.: In looking back at the beginning of my letter I see with regret I have been unkind to the excellent organization which has made possible our friendship with you, which has produced your fine letters, which we are always happy to receive and which we read and re-read. If we have not written as often as we should have it is our fault and we ask
10 you to forgive us.

concern: a matter that is of interest or importance to (sb.)

sincerely: other "greetings" (p. 72, l. 29) are: yours (very) sincerely; to friends: yours, yours ever...

PS.: PS. is short for postscript (added to a letter)

unkind to: not very nice to, hard on ≠ kind, to nice to

friendship: strike a friendship with, make friends with

fine: beautiful, of high quality, enjoyable, splendid

re-read: read over again

it is our fault: (no preposition!) the fault lies with us

forgive: pardon, excuse; please forgive me for being late

Grammaire au fil des nouvelles

Traduisez les phrases suivantes inspirées du texte (le premier chiffre renvoie aux pages, les suivants aux lignes) :

Vous montrez un *tel* intérêt pour moi (place de **a, an**, 72.16).

J'achèterai *tout ce* dont j'ai besoin (72.28).

Il me tarde de recevoir une lettre de vous (gérondif, 72.31).

Les arbres jaunissent, *ceux qui* ne sont pas déjà morts (74.21).

Les gens traversent la rue *pour* être du côté ensoleillé parce que le soleil *n'est plus* trop chaud (emploi de **the**, 74.25, **people** + ...).

Mrs. Bentley *et moi* ne vivons plus ensemble (74.31).

Amanda *ne* portera *plus jamais* de salopettes (76.6).

Je vais les voir une fois *par* semaine (76.13).

Mrs. Bentley m'a demandé de répondre, *ce que* je suis enchanté de faire (76.15).

Écrire des lettres était une activité pour laquelle elle n'était pas très forte (gérondif ; rejet de la préposition, 76.17,18).

Il y a eu beaucoup de remue-ménage (76.23).

Le fait qu'il était dans le pays a suscité un curieux sentiment (gérondif et adjectif possessif, 76.30).

Les États-Unis *furent* pendant de nombreuses années un pays isolé (emploi de **the**, 78.1,2).

Peut-être les prêtres te feront-ils lire l'Iliade (**perhaps** en tête de phrase, contrairement à **never, not only**... ; faire faire, 78.22,23,24).

Ton pays *devrait* être très fier de produire des chefs-d'œuvre que le monde entier peut apprécier (relatif, 78.30).

L'argent que nous te donnons ne représente pas un quart de l'argent que nous *dépensions* en boissons alcoolisées (passé révolu, rupture avec le passé, 80.9).

Mes meilleurs vœux à ta sœur *dont* le bien-être est une si grande préoccupation pour toi (place de **a, an**, 80.30).

THE TELEGRAM

by *Iain Crichton Smith* (born in 1928)

Born on the Isle of Lewis in 1928, Iain Crichton
Smith was educated there and at the University of
Aberdeen. He became a teacher of English in
Clydebank and Dumbarton, and from 1955 at the
High School in Oban until he retired in 1977 to
devote himself to writing full time. He is married
and lives in Argyll.

Iain Crichton Smith is one of Scotland's foremost
living poets and novelists. He has published
numerous volumes of poetry both in English and
Gaelic, some ten novels (among which *Consider the
Lilies,* Canongate Publishing Ltd.) and collections of
short stories including *Survival without Error, The
Black and the Red, Murdo and Other Stories*
published by Gollancz Ltd.

As the author says himself, "*The Telegram* began
because of the fact that during the war messages were
brought by people associated with the Church. I
come from the Highlands of Scotland where the
story is set and many of my stories deal with the idea
of community, threats to the community, and
complex feelings within the community, as between
the two women" (Letter from Tigh na Fuaran,
April 5, 1988).

The two women—one fat and one thin— sat at the window of the thin woman's house drinking tea and looking down the road which ran through the village. They were like two birds, one a fat domestic bird perhaps, the other more aquiline, more gaunt, or, to be precise, more like a buzzard.

It was wartime and though the village appeared quiet, much had gone on in it. Reverberations from a war fought far away had reached it: many of its young men had been
10 killed, or rather drowned, since nearly all of them had joined the navy, and their ships had sunk in seas which they had never seen except on maps which hung on the walls of the local school which they all had at one time or another unwillingly attended. One had been drowned on a destroyer after a leave during which he had told his family that he would never come back again. (Or at least that was the rumour in the village which was still, as it had always been, a superstitious place.) Another had been drowned during the pursuit of the *Bismarck*.

20 What the war had to do with them the people of the village did not know. It came on them as a strange plague, taking their sons away and then killing them, meaninglessly, randomly. They watched the road often for the telegrams.

The telegrams were brought to the houses by the local elder who, clad in black, would walk along the road and then stop at the house to which the telegram was directed. People began to think of the telegram as a strange missile pointed at them from abroad. They did
30 not know what to associate it with, certainly not with God, but it was a weapon of some kind, it picked a door and entered it, and left desolation just like any other weapon.

86

fat: don't eat too much or you'll get fat (≠ thin)
drinking tea: having tea (have a drink, have breakfast...)
the road...ran through the village: note the use of "run"
domestic bird (animal): kept by, living with man (≠ wild)
aquiline: eagle-like, (of nose) hooked □ **gaunt:** meagre, thin as if
ill or hungry □ **a buzzard** is a bird of prey
wartime: the 1914-1918 war; World War II □ **quiet:** calm
gone on: taken place □ **fought:** fight a war, wage a war
had reached it: had come as far as the village
killed...drowned: put to death...had died in water □ **since:** because
navy army... □ **sunk:** submerged in water □ **seas,** like the
Mediterranean □ **map(s):** showing where countries are

unwillingly: perforce □ **attended:** attend a school, go to...
leave: permission to be absent; be *on* leave
at least: in any case, at all events
still: (even) up to now (which continued to be...)

the Bismarck: *the* Queen Elizabeth (a ship) ≠ Queen Elizabeth
to do with...: this has nothing to do with me!
plague: calamity
meaninglessly: in an absurd way; meaningless, senseless
randomly: without plan, haphazardly □ **they watched...:** they
looked down the road wondering if the telegrams were destined for
them □ **brought to:** taken, carried to; bring, brought, brought
elder: official in some Protestant churches □ **clad in black:** dressed
in black, wearing black clothes
think of...: consider, look upon the telegram as...
from abroad: from another country, from a foreign country
God: supernatural being who can control everything
weapon: (nuclear...) weapon, arm □ **kind:** sort □ **picked:** chose,
selected; pick and choose, chose carefully

The two women who watched the street were different, not only physically but socially. For the thin woman's son was a sub-lieutenant in the Navy while the fat woman's son was only an ordinary seaman. The fat woman's son had to salute the thin woman's son. One got more pay than the other, and wore a better uniform. One had been at university and had therefore become an officer, the other had left school at the age of fourteen.

When they looked out the window they could see cows
10 wandering lazily about, but little other movement. The fat woman's cow used to eat the thin woman's washing and she was looking out for it but she couldn't see it. The thin woman was not popular in the village. She was an incomer from another village and had only been in this one for thirty years or so. The fat woman had lived in the village all her days; she was a native. Also the thin woman was ambitious: she had sent her son to university though she only had a widow's pension of ten shillings a week.

As they watched they could see at the far end of the street
20 the tall man in black clothes carrying in his hand a piece of yellow paper. This was a bare village with little colour and therefore the yellow was both strange and unnatural.

The fat woman said: "It's Macleod again."

"I wonder where he's going today."

They were both frightened for he could be coming to their house. And so they watched him and as they watched him they spoke feverishly as if by speaking continually and watching his every move they would be able to keep from themselves whatever plague he was bringing. The thin
30 woman said:

"Don't worry, Sarah, it won't be for you. Donald only left home last week."

street: road (either!) ☐ **different** from each other (from!)

for: because ☐ **son:** male child (daughter, female child)

while: (on the other hand), but, whereas (in contrast)

seaman: a man in the Navy who is not an officer

got more pay: got a better salary, better wages

wore: wear, wore, worn (used for clothes)

therefore: in consequence, consequently

left school...: "at university", go to hospital: no article!

cow(s): big farm animal; a cow gives milk

wandering: going here and there ☐ **lazily:** nonchalantly

washing: clothes drying in the open air, hanging on the line

looking out for it: trying to see the cow

popular: he's very popular with (among) his students

incomer: (pejorative) intruder (not belonging to the village)

thirty years or so: approximately, roughly thirty years

she was a native: she was born in the village

widow: woman whose husband is dead ☐ **ten shillings a week** or per week, every week ☐ **the far end:** the other end; far countries, distant countries (far away)

bare: (here) simple, undecorated, unembellished, unadorned (bare, without clothes on, naked)

Macleod is a typical Scottish family name

I wonder: wonder, ask oneself a question; I wonder if...

frightened: afraid, apprehensive; be frightened of (sth.)

so: consequently ☐ **as...:** during the time that..., while...

feverishly: with much agitation or excitement

his every move: every single movement he made ☐ **to keep** (away) from themselves, to protect themselves from **whatever plague**, from every single plague, from every plague without exception

don't worry: don't be anxious; worry about (sth.) ☐ **only:** not later than; only last week (no article!), only yesterday

"You don't know," said the fat woman, "you don't know." And then she added without thinking, "It's different for the officers."

"Why is it different for the officers?" said the thin woman in an even voice without taking her eyes from the black figure.

"Well, I just thought they're better off," said the fat woman in a confused tone, "they get better food and they get better conditions."

10 "They're still on the ship," said the thin woman who was thinking that the fat woman was very stupid. But then most of them were: they were large, fat and lazy. Most of them could have better afforded to send their sons and daughters to university but they didn't want to be thought of as snobbish.

"They are that," said the fat woman. "But your son is educated," she added irrelevantly. Of course her son didn't salute the thin woman's son if they were both home on leave at the same time. It had happened once they had 20 been. But naturally there was the uneasiness.

"I made sacrifices to have my son educated," said the thin woman. "I lived on a pension of ten shillings a week. I was in nobody's debt. More tea?"

"No thank you," said the fat woman. "He's passed Bessie's house. That means it can't be Roddy. He's safe."

For a terrible moment she realised that she had hoped that the elder would have turned in at Bessie's house. Not that she had anything against either Bessie or Roddy. But 30 still one thought of one's own family first.

The thin woman continued remorselessly as if she were pecking away at something she had pecked at for many

90

you don't know: you can't say for sure
she added: she said also; addition ≠ subtraction; add ≠ subtract

even: regular and unchanging, not showing emotion
figure: shape or form of the human body, contour
they're better off: they have better living conditions
tone: tone of voice □ **food:** what can be eaten; feed (fed, fed), give food; underfed, who does not get enough food
they're still on the ship: they are on the ship all the same, like ordinary seamen; still, however, yet, nevertheless
large: big, corpulent □ **lazy:** doing little work, inactive
afforded: afford, be able to pay for
to be thought of as snobbish: (passive)... they didn't want people to think they were snobbish; a snob
they are that: they are snobbish (in actual fact)
irrelevantly: irrelevant, having no relation with (what was said before) (≠ relevant) □ **salute** (an officer), make a salute
happened: taken place □ **once they had been:** on one occasion when they had come to the village □ **uneasiness:** embarrassment

lived on a pension...: live on fruit... (on!) □ **I was in nobody's debt:** I did not owe anybody any money; be in debt ≠ be out of debt; run into debt, begin to owe money
means: mean, signify, indicate; mean, meant, meant; meaning
safe: out of danger (not "killed" or "drowned"), spared
realised: was conscious, understood □ **hoped:** expected and desired; hope, feeling of confidence in the future; we live in hope(s) of a better world; in the hope of doing (sth.)
one thought of one's own (personal) **family:** people in general...
remorselessly: without remorse □ **were:** more formal than was
pecking: like a bird with its beak □ **away:** continuously

years. "The teacher told me to send Iain to University. He came to see me. I had no thought of sending him before he came. 'Send your son to university,' he said to me. 'He's got a good head on him.' And I'll tell you, Sarah, I had to save every penny. Ten shillings isn't much. When did you see me with good clothes in the church?"

"That's true," said the fat woman absently. "We have to make sacrifices." It was difficult to know what she was 10 thinking of—the whale meat or the saccharines? Or the lack of clothes? Her mind was vague and diffused except when she was thinking about herself.

The thin woman continued: "Many's the night I used to sit here in this room and knit clothes for him when he was young. I even knitted trousers for him. And for all I know he may marry an English girl and where will I be? He might go and work in England. He was staying in a house there at Christmas. He met a girl at a dance and he found out later that her father was a mayor. I'm sure 20 she smokes and drinks. And he might not give me anything after all I've done for him."

"Donald spends all his money," said the fat woman. "He never sends me anything. When he comes home on leave he's never in the house. But I don't mind. He was always like that. Meeting strange people and buying them drinks. It's his nature and he can't go against his nature. He's passed the Smiths. That means Tommy's all right."

There were only another three houses before he would 30 reach her own, and then the last one was the one where she was sitting.

"I think I'll take a cup of tea," she said. And then, "I'm

92

send: send (sb.) to university, to school; send, sent, sent

I had no thought of...: I did not envisage or contemplate sending him...; thought, idea, notion; think, thought, thought

he's got a good head on him: (fam.) he's intelligent, clever

save every penny: economize, scrimp, skimp

with good clothes: well-dressed, with fine clothes on

church: building where people attend religious services

true: correct, right □ **absently:** inattentively, absent-mindedly

to make sacrifices: make sacrifices (not do!)

whale: *baleine* □ **meat:** parts of animals used as food

lack: absence or need, want ≠ profusion □ **mind:** intellect; he has a good mind, he's intelligent

many's the night...: I spent so many nights sitting...

knit: make clothes with wool and long needles

even (if it is a lot of work) □ **trousers:** two-legged piece of clothing (like jeans) □ **for all I know:** as far as I know, God knows □ **where will...:** will be lost without him

found out: discovered □ **mayor:** man elected to be head of town

she smokes (cigarettes) **and drinks:** both actions regarded as immoral! (notice that this Scottish lady does not like England very much either: see line 16, 17) □ **spend:** spend money on (sth.) (notice the preposition); spend, spent, spent

mind: attach importance to (sth.) □ **meeting strange people...:** mixing with people he did not know (strangers), treating them to drinks in the pub □ **the Smiths:** with an *s*!

all right: or alright (one l!), "safe" (p. 90 l. 26)

another three houses: three other houses, three more houses

reach her own (house): come up to her own □ **last:** ≠ first; last but one (that comes just before the last)

take a cup of tea: or have... (a drink, a meal (p. 86 l. 2))

sorry about the cow." But no matter how you tried you never could like the thin woman. She was always putting on airs. Mayor indeed. Sending her son to university. Why did she want to be better than anyone else? Saving and scrimping all the time. And everybody said that her son wasn't as clever as all that. He had failed some of his exams too. Her own Donald was just as clever and could have gone to university but he was too fond of fishing and being out with the boys.

10   As she drank her tea her heart was beating and she was frightened and she didn't know what to talk about and yet she wanted to talk. She liked talking, after all what else was there to do? But the thin woman didn't gossip much. You couldn't feel at ease with her, you had the idea all the time that she was thinking about something else.

The thin woman came and sat down beside her.

"Did you hear," said the fat woman, "that Malcolm Mackay was up on a drunken charge? He smashed his car, so they say. It was in the black-out."

20   "I didn't hear that," said the thin woman.

"It was coming home last night with the meat. He had it in the van and he smashed it at the burn. But they say he's all right. I don't know how they kept him out of the war. They said it was his heart but there was nothing wrong with his heart. Everyone knows it was influence. What's wrong with his heart if he can drink and smash a car?"

The thin woman drank her tea very delicately. She used to be away on service a long time before she was married 30 and she had a dainty way of doing things. She sipped her tea, her little finger elegantly curled in an irritating way.

"Why do you keep your finger like that?" said the fat

no matter...: even if you tried very hard (to like...), however hard you tried □ **putting on airs** to make people think she was important

mayor indeed: (ironical) was she any better for that? (if her son went out with a mayor's daughter)

scrimp: save slowly, with difficulty, by living poorly, skimp

clever: intelligent, smart □ **failed:** fail an exam ≠ pass an exam (no preposition!); failure ≠ success

fond of: be fond of (sth.), like (sth.) very much

fishing fish, try to catch fish or fishes (animals in water)

beating: (hard), thumping (because she was anxious)

talk: speak; talk politics (no preposition!); talk, conversation, discussion; talkative, fond of talking

gossip: talk about other people's private lives in detail

at ease: ≠ ill at ease, embarrassed, nervous, uncomfortable

something else: another thing; somebody else, somewhere else...

beside her: near her, next to her, by her side

did you hear (people say...), were you told that...?

on a drunken charge: accused of drinking □ **smashed...:** had his car ruined in an accident □ **black out:** period of darkness enforced during wartime as a protection against air attack

van: large car for carrying merchandise □ **burn:** small stream or river in Scotland □ **kept him out...:** exempted him from...

heart: heart attack; cardiac unit (in a hospital) □ **nothing wrong with...:** he had no heart disease

influence: use one's influence with (sb.) to get (sth.); influential politicians; string pulling (slang for "influence")

used to: be in the habit of + ing

be on service: be employed as a domestic servant

dainty: (too) delicate, affected □ **sipped:** sip, drink a very small quantity at a time □ **curled:** curved (in a half-circle)

keep: cause to stay in a certain position; keep, kept, kept

woman suddenly.

"Like what?"

The fat woman demonstrated.

"Oh, it was the way I saw the guests drinking tea in the hotels when I was on service. They always drank like that."

"He's passed the Stewarts," said the fat woman. Two houses to go. They looked at each other wildly. It must be one of them. Surely. They could see the elder quite
10 clearly now, walking very stiff, very upright, wearing his black hat. He walked in a stately dignified manner, eyes straight ahead of him.

"He's proud of what he's doing," said the fat woman suddenly. "You'd think he was proud of it. Knowing before anyone else. And he himself was never in the war."

"Yes," said the thin woman, "it gives him a position." They watched him. They both knew him well. He was a stiff, quiet man who kept himself to
20 himself, more than ever now. He didn't mix with people and he always carried the Bible into the pulpit for the minister.

"They say his wife had one of her fits again," said the fat woman viciously. He had passed the Murrays. The next house was her own. She sat perfectly still. Oh, pray God it wasn't hers.

And yet it must be hers. Surely it must be hers. She had dreamt of this happening, her son drowning in the Atlantic ocean, her own child whom she had reared, whom
30 she had seen going to play football in his green jersey and white shorts, whom she had seen running home from school. She could see him drowning but she couldn't

suddenly: quickly, unexpectedly, all of a sudden; sudden, done quickly, happening unexpectedly
demonstrated: showed her by curling her own little finger
way: manner □ **guest(s):** person staying at a hotel
I was on service: notice the preposition "on"

two (more) houses to go before the elder reached their own
wildly: uncontrollably frightened, looking mad with fright
quite clearly: very distinctly; quite, not quiet! (calm)
stiff: rigid, firm, strict □ **upright:** erect, not at all bent
stately: imposing, impressive, majestic, solemn
straight: directly □ **ahead of him:** in front of him
proud: having too much pride or self-satisfaction
you'd think...: by the look of him people would think... □ **knowing anyone else** who was killed, which villager

a (social) position in relation to others, status
they both knew: or both of them knew, both women knew
quiet: who kept silent (≠ noisy) □ **who kept himself to himself:** who was distant (socially), who "didn't mix with other people"
pulpit: place in church used by clergymen for sermons
minister: Christian clergyman
fit(s): sudden attack of hysteria with violent movements
viciously: cruelly, ferociously □ **next:** coming immediately after in order, following □ **pray God it was not hers:** please God, let it be (sb.) else's house; pray, talk to God, thanking him or asking him for (sth.); prayer, act of praying or the words used □ **she had dreamt...:** she had seen in her sleep; dream of (sth.)
reared: brought up, looked after, raised (since he was a baby)
jersey: knitted piece of clothing, pullover
running home: come home, go home... (no preposition!)
drown: drown (no reflexive pronoun!), get drowned

make out the name of the ship. She had never seen a really big ship and what she imagined was more like the mailboat than a cruiser. Her son couldn't drown out there for no reason that she could understand. God couldn't do that to people. It was impossible. God was kinder than that. God helped you in your sore trouble. She began to mutter a prayer over and over. She said it quickly like the Catholics, O God save my son O God save my son O God save my son. She was ashamed of prattling in that way as

10 if she was counting beads but she couldn't stop herself, and on top of that she would soon cry. She knew it and she didn't want to cry in front of that woman, that foreigner. It would be weakness. She felt the arm of the thin woman around her shoulders, the thin arm, and it was like first love, it was like the time Murdo had taken her hand in his when they were coming home from the dance, such an innocent gesture, such a spontaneous gesture. So unexpected, so strange, so much a gift. She was crying and she couldn't look...

20 "He has passed your house," said the thin woman in a distant firm voice, and she looked up. He was walking along and he had indeed passed her house. She wanted to stand up and dance all round the kitchen, all fifteen stone of her, and shout and cry and sing a song but then she stopped. She couldn't do that. How could she do that when it must be the thin woman's son? There was no other house. The thin woman was looking out at the elder, her lips pressed closely together, white and bloodless. Where had she learnt that self-control? She wasn't crying or

30 shaking. She was looking out at something she had always dreaded but she wasn't going to cry or surrender or give herself away to anyone.

make out: see or read with difficulty, decipher

mailboat: boat carrying mail (letters...) to the island

cruiser: large fast warship □ **out there:** far away

reason: there is no reason why... (notice "why")

kinder: better; kind, kind-hearted, good-hearted (≠ cruel)

sore trouble: severe, terrible difficulty, great misfortune

mutter (in a low indistinct voice) □ **over and over** (again): repeatedly □ **save:** make safe from danger, spare, protect (from)

was ashamed: felt shame (*honte*) □ **prattling:** talking continuously

counting (from 1 to...) □ **beads:** *grains de chapelet*

on top...: in addition □ **soon:** before long □ **cry:** weep (her eyes would fill with tears)

foreigner: one from another country □ **weakness:** ≠ firmess, fortitude □ **shoulder(s):** part of body joining arm to trunk

gesture: make a gesture (not do!)

strange: unknown to her □ **so much a gift:** such a (wonderful) gift; a gift, a present; give, gave, given □ **look** or see (through her tears) where the elder was exactly

she looked up: she raised her eyes; look up ≠ look down

indeed: in fact □ **she wanted...:** she felt like... dancing...

kitchen: room where food is cooked □ **fifteen stone** (no s!): = 95,25 kg; 1 stone = 6,35 kg □ **shout** (for joy): cry out in a loud (≠ low) voice □ **she stopped** (herself from, she refrained herself from even thinking of dancing, singing...) □ **no other house:** (than hers); other... *than;* same... *as*

lip(s): *lèvre* □ **closely:** firmly, tightly □ **bloodless:** pale (for strong emotion), without blood (red liquid in body)

shaking: trembling; shake, shook, shaken

dreaded: been afraid of, feared □ **surrender:** abandon herself to despair, give up □ **give herself away:** reveal her personality, her secret

And at that moment the fat woman saw. She saw the years of discipline, she remembered how thin and unfed and pale the thin woman had always looked, how sometimes she had had to borrow money, even a shilling to buy food. She saw what it must have been like to be a widow bringing up a son in a village not her own. She saw it so clearly that she was astounded. It was as if she had an extra vision, as if the air itself brought the past with all its details nearer. The number of times the thin woman had
10 been ill and people had said that she was weak and useless. She looked down at the thin woman's arm. It was so shrivelled, and dry.

And the elder walked on. A few yards now till he reached the plank. But the thin woman hadn't cried. She was steady and still, her lips still compressed, sitting upright in her chair. And, miracle of miracles, the elder passed the plank and walked straight on.

They looked at each other. What did it all mean? Where was the elder going, clutching his telegram
20 in his hand, walking like a man in a daze? There were no other houses so where was he going? They drank their tea in silence, turning away from each other. The fat woman said, "I must be going." They parted for the moment without speaking. The thin woman still sat at the window looking out. Once or twice the fat woman made as if to turn back as if she had something to say, some message to pass on, but she didn't. She walked away.

It wasn't till later that night that they discovered what had happened. The elder had a telegram directed to himself,
30 to tell him of the drowning of his own son. He should never have seen it just like that, but there had been a mistake at the post office, owing to the fact that there were two boys

100

saw: knew, realized, understood
unfed: insufficiently fed; feed, fed, fed, give food (sth. to eat) to
looked: seemed, appeared (to be)
borrow: get (sth.) after promising to return it □ **even...:** as little as a shilling; £ 1 (one pound) = 20 shillings
not her own: where she was not born; she did not belong there
astounded: shocked with surprise
extra: additional, supplementary □ **vision:** sight

ill: unwell, in bad health (because she was "unfed")
useless: good for nothing, worthless
shrivelled: made smaller (through illness, old age), wasted
walked on: continued to walk, went on his way □ **yard(s):** 91,44 cm
plank: piece of wood across the ditch (*fossé*) (from the house to the road) □ **steady:** ≠ shaking □ **still:** without any movement, motionless □ **upright:** ≠ bent, limp (p. 96 l. 10)

they looked at each other or one another (either!)
mean: signify, indicate □ **clutching:** holding firmly, seizing
in a daze or dazed, unable to think or feel clearly (after an accident... after hearing terrible news), stupefied, stunned
turning away from each other: refusing to look at each other
they parted: part, separate, no longer be together
still: indicates continuation (≠ still, adjective p. 86, l. 17)
once, twice, three times... □ **made as if to...:** was about to
turn back: no reflexive pronoun!

till: two l's!; until (one l!) □ **later:** late ≠ early
directed to himself: destined for himself
his own son: (emphatic for "his son"), not anybody else's
mistake: error, (sth.) done wrong: make a mistake (not do!)
owing to the fact: due to the fact, because of...

in the village with the same name. His walk through the village was a somnambulistic wandering. He didn't want to go home and tell his wife what had happened. He was walking along not knowing where he was going when later he was stopped half way to the next village. Perhaps he was going in search of his son. Altogether he had walked six miles. The telegram was crushed in his fingers and so sweaty that they could hardly make out the writing.

name: family name or surname; first name or Christian name
wandering: wander, go about without any special destination
tell his wife: tell (sb. sth. or tell sth. to sb.); tell, told, told

half way: at an equal distance (between the two villages)
in search of: looking for, trying to find □ **altogether:** in all
miles: 1 mile = 1,609 m □ **crushed:** (com)pressed (into a ball)
sweaty: covered in sweat (*sueur*) □ **hardly:** scarcely, barely

Grammaire au fil des nouvelles

Traduisez les phrases suivantes inspirées du texte (le premier chiffre renvoie aux pages, les suivants aux lignes) :

Il marchait le long de la route et s'arrêtait devant la maison à laquelle le télégramme était destiné (comportement prévisible dans le passé, sens dit fréquentatif de ... 86.26).

Le fils de la grosse dame *devait* saluer le fils de la femme maigre (substituts des auxiliaires modaux, 88.4).

L'un était allé à *l'*université (institution, 88.6).

La vache mangeait le linge (passé révolu, 88.11).

Elle *était* dans ce village *depuis* trente ans (88.14).

Le jaune était *à la fois* étrange et irréel (88.22).

Donald n'a quitté la maison que *la semaine dernière* (emploi de **the**, 88.32).

Elles ne voulaient pas passer pour des snobs (proposition infinitive ; voie passive avec verbe à particule, 90.14).

J'ai consenti des sacrifices pour *faire éduquer* mon enfant (90.21).

On pensait d'abord à sa propre famille (place de l'adverbe, 90.30).

*Il se peut qu'*il épouse *une Anglaise. Il se pourrait qu'*il aille travailler en Angleterre (92.16,17).

Il n'envoie jamais rien (**some, any, no** et composés, 92.23).

Il a passé les Smi*th*, les Stuar*t*, les Murra*y* (pluriel des noms de famille, 92.27 ; 96.7,24).

On avait beau essayer, *on* ne pouvait aimer la femme maigre (94.1).

Son Donald *aurait pu* aller à l'université (94.8).

Qu'y avait-il d'*autre* à faire... Quelque chose d'*autre*... (94.12,13,15).

Elles se regardèrent, affolées (réciprocité, 96.8)

Il portait toujours la Bible (place de l'adverbe, 96.21)

Oh, Dieu fasse que ce ne soit pas *le sien* (96.26).

Elle comprit ce que cela *avait dû être* (100.5). Il n'aurait jamais *dû voir* le télégramme comme ça (100.30).

Peut-être allait-il à la recherche de son père (**perhaps**, en tête de phrase, contrairement à **never, not only**... 102.5).

"IN AFFECTION AND ESTEEM"

by Mary Webb (1888-1927)

Mary Webb is the author of a number of country novels set in Shropshire. The best known are *Precious Bane, Gone to Earth* and *Sarn*. They are, to a certain extent, reminiscent of Thomas Hardy's *Tess of the D'Urbervilles* with their wild heroines, their scenes of rustic violence and their nature-poetry.

In Affection and Esteem is taken from *Armour Wherein He Trusted and Other Stories*.

Miss Myrtle Brown had never received the gift of a box or a bouquet of flowers. She used to think, as she trudged away to the underground station every day, to go and stitch buttonholes in a big London shop, that it would have been nice if, on one of her late returns, she had found a bunch of roses—red, with thick, lustrous petals, deeply sweet, or white, with their rare fragrance—awaiting her on her table. It was, of course, an impossible dream. She ought to be glad enough to have a table at all, and a loaf to put
10 on it. She ought to be grateful to those above for letting her have a roof over her head.

"You might," she apostrophized herself, as she lit her gas-ring and put on the kettle, "not *have* a penny for this slot. You might, Myrtle Brown, not *have* a spoonful of tea to put in this pot. Be thankful!"

And she was thankful to Providence, to her landlady, to her employer, who sweated his workers, to the baker for bringing her loaf, to the milkman for leaving her half a pint of milk on Sundays, to the landlady's cat for refraining
20 from drinking it.

Yet she could not help thinking, when she put out her light and lay down, of the wonderful moment if she ever *did* receive a bouquet.

Think of unpacking the box! Think of seeing on the outside, 'Cut Flowers. Immediate', undoing the string, taking off the paper, lifting the lid!

What then? Ah, violets, perhaps, or roses; lilies of the valley; lilac or pale pink peonies or mimosa with its warm sweetness.
30 The little room would be like a greenhouse—like one of the beautiful greenhouses at Kew. She would borrow jam-pots from the landlady, and it would take all evening to

gift: present; give (sb. sth.), present (sb. with sth.)

trudged: walked slowly, with effort, plodded

underground: tube, subway (Am.), métro □ **stitch:** sew *(coudre)*

buttonhole(s): hole (s) into which buttons fit

on... her late returns: on coming back late □ **bunch:** bouquet

thick: ≠ thin □ **lustrous:** shining □ **deeply sweet:** very sweet smelling

fragrance: perfume □ **awaiting her:** waiting for her

of course: naturally □ **dream:** (sth.) one sees during sleep

glad... happy just to have a table □ **loaf:** loaf of bread

grateful: full of gratitude, thankful □ **those above:** (in Paradise),
providence □ **roof:** top covering of a house

lit: put a flame to and cause to burn; light, lit, lit

gas-ring: gas cooker □ **kettle:** metal vessel for boiling water

slot: opening to insert penny in □ **spoonful:** what a spoon
can hold; cupful, glassful, handful... □ **pot:** teapot, coffee pot...

landlady: the lady she pays every month for her room

sweated...: made them work hard for little money □ **baker:** one
who makes bread □ **half a pint:** 1 pint = 0,57 litre

refraining from drinking it: abstaining from drinking it

help thinking: refrain from thinking □ **put out her light:** turned off
the electricity, switched off □ **lay down:** (in bed) lie, lay, lain □ **...did
receive:** if, in fact, she received

think of unpacking: imagine taking the flowers out of...

outside: exterior □ **immediate:** urgent □ **string:** fine cord

lifting the lid: taking up, raising the cover to open the box

lilies of the valley: flowers associated with May 1st

lilac: *lilas* □ **pink:** pale red □ **peonies:** peony *(pivoine)*

warm sweetness: nice warm smell

greenhouse: glass building for growing plants, flowers

Kew (Botanical Gardens) □ **borrow jam pots:** take for some time
and give back; borrow money from (sb.); jam is made from fruit

arrange them. And the room would be wonderful—like heaven.

To wake, slowly and luxuriously, on a Sunday morning, into that company—what bliss!

She might, of course, out of her weekly wage, buy a bunch of flowers. She did occasionally. But that was not quite the perfect thing, not quite what she desired. The centre of all the wonder was to be the little bit of pasteboard with her name on it, and the sender's name, and perhaps a

10 few words of greeting. She had heard that this was the custom in sending a bouquet to anyone—a great actress or a prima donna. And on birthdays it was customary, and at funerals.

Birthdays! Suppose, now, she received such a parcel on her birthday. She had had so many birthdays, and they had all been so very much alike. A tomato with her tea, perhaps, and a cinema afterwards. Once it had been a pantomime, the landlady having been given a ticket, and having passed it on in consideration of some help with

20 needlework.

Always in her heart was the longing for some great pageant, some splendid gift of radiance. How she would enjoy it! But nobody seemed anxious to inaugurate any pageant. And at last, on a bleak winter day when everything had gone wrong and she had been quite unable to be grateful to anybody, she made a reckless decision. She would provide a pageant for herself. Before she began to save up for the rainy day, she would save up for the pageant.

30 "After that," she remarked, carefully putting crumbs on the window-sill for the birds, "you'll be quiet. You'll be truly thankful, Myrtle Brown."

wonderful: marvellous; the seven wonders of the world
heaven: paradise ≠ hell; what heavenly weather! (wonderful)
wake: stop sleeping □ **luxuriously:** as if rich and comfortable
bliss: complete happiness as if one were in heaven, felicity
weekly wage: salary earned every week; weekly, daily, monthly
occasionally: from time to time, now and then
quite: entirely, completely; I don't quite understand
bit (piece) of pasteboard (cardboard): small card
sender: one who sends a letter...; send, sent, sent ≠ receive
greeting: good wishes; Christmas greetings; greeting(s) card
custom: tradition, habit; customary, habitual, usual
prima donna: leading woman singer in opera
funeral(s): burial; bury a dead person in a tomb
such a parcel: a parcel (packet) like that

alike: similar, like one another □ **tea:** five o'clock meal
afterwards: after that □ **once:** one day; once upon a time
pantomime: comic musical play for children □ **having been given:**
(passive!) having received □ **in consideration of:** in return for
needlework: sewing, work with a needle *(aiguille)*
the longing for: the strong wish for; long for, desire ardently
pageant: great feast □ **radiance:** brilliance, brightness
enjoy it: love it □ **anxious:** strongly desirous to, eager to
at (long) last: in the end □ **bleak:** cold and grey, dreary
had gone wrong in an unpleasant way, not as you wish
reckless: very imprudent, rash, wild
provide a pageant for herself: give herself a pageant
save up: economize □ **the rainy day:** time of (pecuniary) need

carefully: with care, attention □ **crumbs:** very small bits of bread
window-sill: *rebord de fenêtre* □ **you'll be quiet:** you'll calm down;
quiet, calm ≠ excited □ **truly:** sincerely

She began to scrimp and save.   Week by week the little hoard increased.   A halfpenny here and a penny there—it was wonderful how soon she amassed a shilling.   So great was her determination that, before her next birthday, she had got together two pounds.

"It's a wild and wicked thing to spend two pounds on what neither feeds nor clothes", she said.   She knew it would be impossible to tell the landlady.   She would never hear the last of it.   No! It must be a dead secret.   Nobody
10 must know where those flowers came from.   What was the word people used when you were not to know the name?

'Anon'.   Yes.   The flowers must be 'anon'.   There was a little shop at Covent Garden where they would sell retail.   Wonderful things were heaped in hampers.   She would go there on the day before her birthday.

She was radiant as she surveyed early London from the bus.   She descended at Covent Garden, walking through the piled crates of greenstuff, the casks of fruit, the bursting sacks of potatoes.   The shopkeeper was busy.   He saw a
20 shabby little woman with an expression of mingled rapture and anxiety.

"I want some flowers.   Good flowers.   They are to be packed and sent to a lady I know, tonight."

"Violets?"

"Yes, violets and tuberoses and lilies and pheasant-eye and maidenhair and mimosa and a few dozen roses."

"Wait a minute! Wait a minute! I suppose you know they'll cost you a pretty penny."

"I can pay for what I order," said Miss Brown with
30 hauteur.   "Write down what I say, add it up as you go on, put down box and postage, and I'll pay."

The shopkeeper did as he was told.

scrimp: save slowly, with difficulty by living poorly, skimp
hoard: money amassed; hoard (up), amass, save □ **increased:** augmented ≠ decreased □ **soon:** quickly □ **shilling:** (until) 1971 1/20 of a pound = 5 p (5 pence in present system) □ **next:** coming immediately after, following □ **got together:** amassed
wild: reckless, mad, foolish □ **wicked:** bad, immoral, foolish
what neither feeds nor clothes: or neither food nor clothes; feed: give food (victuals) to; clothe: put clothes on
the last...: the landlady would always talk about it □ **dead secret:** top secret; dead (here), complete; a dead calm
you were not to know: (because it had been arranged in advance); he is to come tomorrow □ **anon:** anonymous; anonymity
Covent Garden: flower, fruit and vegetable market in London
sell retail: sell to the public □ **heaped:** piled □ **hamper(s):** large basket with lids, usually used for carrying food
radiant: radiant with joy □ **surveyed:** looked round □ **early London:** London in the morning □ **descended:** got off the bus
crate(s), cask(s): container(s) □ **greenstuff:** vegetables □ **bursting:** full up to the point of bursting; burst, break open suddenly
shabby: poorly dressed □ **mingled:** mixed □ **rapture;** great joy, go into raptures, become extremely happy □ **anxiety:** apprehension, fright, fear; anxious, apprehensive □ **they are to be packed:** they must be packed, put into a box (≠ unpack)

tuberose(s): *tubéreuse* □ **lilies:** lily, *lys* □ **pheasant-eye:** a type of narcissus □ **maidenhair:** *capillaire* □ **dozen:** twelve
wait: wait for (sb.); I'll be waiting for you in the hall
cost: costly, expensive □ **a pretty penny:** a lot of money
order: ask; order a meal in a restaurant, order a taxi
hauteur: arrogance, pride □ **add:** addition ≠ subtraction
put down: write down □ **postage:** cost of sending letters, parcels by the post □ **as he was told** (to do by Myrtle Brown)

Miss Brown went from flower to flower, like a sad-coloured butterfly, softly touching a petal, softly sniffing a rose. The shopkeeper, realizing that something unusual was afoot, gave generous measure. At last the order was complete, the address given, the money—all the two pounds—paid.

"Any card enclosed?" queried the shopman.

Triumphantly Miss Brown produced one. 'In affection and esteem.'

10 "A good friend, likely?" queried the shopman.

"Almost my only friend," replied Miss Brown.

Through Covent Garden's peculiarly glutinous mud she went in a beatitude, worked in a beatitude, went home in a dream.

She slept brokenly, as children do on Christmas Eve, and woke early, listening for the postman's ring.

Hark! Yes! A ring.

But the landlady did not come up. It must have been only the milkman. Another wait. Another ring. No
20 footsteps. The baker, she surmised.

Where was the postman? He was very late. If he only knew, how quick he would have been!

Another pause. An hour. Nothing. It was long past his time. She went down.

"Postman?" said the landlady, "why, the postman's been gone above an hour! Parcel? No, nothing for you. There did come a parcel for Miss Brown, but it was a great expensive box with 'Cut Flowers' on it, so I knew it wasn't for you and I sent it straight to Miss Elvira Brown the
30 actress, who used to lodge here. *She* was always getting stacks of flowers, so I knew it was for her."

sad-coloured: with sad colours; sad ≠ brilliant, bright
butterfly: *papillon* □ **softly:** delicately, gently □ **sniffing:** smelling
realizing: understanding □ **unusual:** exceptional
afoot: happening, in progress □ **at last:** in the end □ **order:** give an
order (in a shop, a restaurant), order (a meal...) (p. 110, l. 29)
pound(s): (today) 1 pound (£ 1) = 100 p (pence)
enclosed: (to be) put (in the box, in an envelope) □ **queried:** asked
produced: showed suddenly like a magician out of a hat
esteem: hold (sb.) in high esteem; be much loved and esteemed
likely: probably; most likely, very likely
almost: practically □ **only:** an only child □ **replied:** answered
peculiarly: exceptionally □ **glutinous:** sticky □ **mud:** in rainy
weather you have mud on your shoes; muddy

brokenly: intermittently, on and off □ **Christmas Eve:** evening
before Christmas □ **listening for the postman's ring:** expecting to
hear the postman pressing the door bell □ **hark!:** listen!
come up: come upstairs □ **it must have been:** surely, no doubt it was
wait: (noun!) a ten minutes' wait
footstep(s): sound of steps of (sb.) walking □ **surmised:** supposed
postman: mailman; (Am.) post, mail: letters, postcards, parcels
delivered by the postman □ **quick:** double quick
pause: silence □ **it was long past his time:** it was long after
the postman's usual time □ **went down:** went downstairs
why: (expressing surprise) oh, but! (≠ why?)
's been gone above an hour: left here more than an hour ago
there did come...: in fact a parcel came □ **great:** big, large
expensive: ≠ inexpensive, cheap □ **I knew:** I understood, I gathered
straight to: directly to
lodge: live as a lodger, paying for room(s) in sb's house
stacks of: (fam.) lots of □ **so:** in consequence, consequently

Grammaire au fil des nouvelles

Traduisez les phrases suivantes inspirées du texte (le premier chiffre renvoie aux pages, les suivants aux lignes) :

Elle se disait que cela *aurait été* merveilleux si elle avait trouvé un bouquet de roses sur sa table (passé révolu ; concordance des temps, 106.2).

Elle *devrait* être assez contente d'avoir seulement une table (place de **enough** avec adjectifs et adverbes, 106.8,9).

Elle était reconnaissante envers *sa* logeuse, envers *son* employeur *qui* exploitait *ses* ouvriers (accord du possessif, 106.16).

Elle ne pouvait s'empêcher de penser à ce moment merveilleux, si elle recevait bel et bien un bouquet... Il est bien arrivé un colis pour Miss Brown (forme d'insistance, 106.21 et 112.26,27).

Elle avait eu *tant* d'anniversaires (**much** ou **many**? 108.15).

... la logeuse ayant reçu un billet... Le marchand fit ce qu'on lui dit (voix passive avec **give, offer, buy, sell, teach, tell, ask**... 108.18 et 110.32).

Personne ne *devait* savoir d'où venaient ces fleurs (rejet de la préposition, 110.10).

Quel était le mot que *les* gens employaient quand on ne *devait* pas connaître le nom?... Les fleurs *doivent* être envoyées à une dame *que* je connais (futur de projet, 110.11,22).

Cela *avait dû être* seulement le laitier... (auxiliaire modal, 112.18).

Comme il se serait dépêché! (**how** exclamatif, 112.22).

Je l'ai envoyé directement à Miss Elvira Brown, l'actrice *qui* habitait ici autrefois (passé révolu : pour opposer ce qui était à ce qui n'est plus ; voir aussi 112.29).

THE LUNCHEON

by W.Somerset Maugham (1874-1965)

W. Somerset Maugham lived in Paris until he was ten. He was educated at King's School, Canterbury and at Heidelberg University. He received his medical training at St. Thomas's Hospital in London. He had acquired a cosmopolitan outlook when he began writing and his autobiographical novel *Of Human Bondage* (1915) reflected much of his disillusionment with European life. Other major works are *The Moon and Sixpence* (1919), *Cakes and Ales* (1930), *The Razor's Edge* (1944) with which Maugham captured a wider public than ever before. His numerous short stories are collected in four volumes by Penguin Books Limited.

More than anything else, Maugham appears as a realist, sceptical of abstractions. His works are full of dry sardonic humour.

I caught sight of her at the play and in answer to her beckoning I went over during the interval and sat down beside her. It was long since I had last seen her and if someone had not mentioned her name I hardly think I would have recognised her. She addressed me brightly.

"Well, it's many years since we first met. How time does fly! We're none of us getting any younger. Do you remember the first time I saw you? You asked me to luncheon."

10   Did I remember?

It was twenty years ago and I was living in Paris. I had a tiny apartment in the Latin Quarter overlooking a cemetery and I was earning barely enough money to keep body and soul together. She had read a book of mine and had written to me about it. I answered, thanking her, and presently I received from her another letter saying she was passing through Paris and would like to have a chat with me; but her time was limited and the only free moment she had was on the following Thursday; she was spending the
20   morning at the Luxembourg and would I give her a little luncheon at Foyot's afterwards? Foyot's is a restaurant at which the French senators eat and it was so far beyond my means that I had never even thought of going there. But I was flattered and I was too young to have learned to say no to a woman. (Few men, I may add, learn this until they are too old to make it of any consequence to a woman what they say.) I had eighty francs (gold francs) to last me the rest of the month and a modest luncheon should not cost more than fifteen. If I cut out coffee for the next two
30   weeks I could manage well enough.

I answered that I would meet my friend—by correspondence—at Foyot's on Thursday at half-past twelve. She

116

caught sight of: saw □ **play** like Hamlet..., theatre drama
beckoning: sign with the hand □ **interval:** pause between two parts
of a play □ **beside:** near, next to
I hardly think: I don't really think; hardly, only just
brightly: gaily; bright, gay, cheerful, happy
we first met: we met for the first time; meet, met, met
fly: pass quickly; time flies! □ **get**+adjective: become
asked me to...: ask (sb.) to lunch, invite (sb.) to lunch
luncheon: more formal word than lunch
did I remember?: and how! needless to say I did remember!

tiny: very small □ **apartment:** room, (Am.) flat □ **overlooking:** with
a view of □ **earning** money (not win!) □ **barely:** hardly
keep body and soul together: survive □ **...of mine:** one of my...

presently: very soon; (be careful! at present, now)
chat: friendly informal conversation; to chat
free: without work; a businessman has little free time
following: coming immediately after, next; follow, come after
would I give her: she asked in her letter if "I would give her"
afterwards: after that, later
so far...: much too expensive for me □ **beyond:** exceeding the limit
of my (financial) **means** (resources) □ **even:** even a child can do that
flattered: flattering; flattery
add: ≠ subtract; addition ≠ subtraction
it (idiomatic, expletive) = "what they say" □ **consequence:**
importance □ **gold:** precious yellow metal □ **last:** be sufficient (for);
we have enough food to last three days □ **cost:** cost, cost, cost
cut out: (fam.) suppressed; cut out tobacco, stop smoking
manage: succeed in living (on little money)
I answered: I replied; an answer, a reply
at Foyot's (restaurant), at the baker's (shop), at John's (house)

was not so young as I expected and in appearance imposing rather than attractive. She was in fact a woman of forty (a charming age, but not one that excites a sudden and devastating passion at first sight), and she gave me the impression of having more teeth, white and large and even, than were necessary for any practical purpose. She was talkative, but since she seemed inclined to talk about me I was prepared to be an attentive listener.

I was startled when the bill of fare was brought, for the
10 prices were a great deal higher than I had anticipated. But she reassured me.

"I never eat anything for luncheon", she said.

"Oh, don't say that!" I answered generously.

"I never eat more than one thing. I think people eat far too much nowadays. A little fish, perhaps. I wonder if they have any salmon."

Well, it was early in the year for salmon and it was not on the bill of fare, but I asked the waiter if there was any. Yes, a beautiful salmon had just come in, it was the
20 first they had had. I ordered it for my guest. The waiter asked her if she would have something while it was being cooked. "No", she answered, "I never eat more than one thing. Unless you had a little caviare. I never mind caviare."

My heart sank a little. I knew I could not afford caviare, but I could not very well tell her that. I told the waiter by all means to bring caviare. For myself I chose the cheapest dish on the menu and that was a mutton chop.

"I think you're unwise to eat meat," she said. "I don't
30 know how you can expect to work after eating heavy things like chops. I don't believe in overloading my stomach."

Then came the question of drink.

expected: anticipated; he expected her to be younger
attractive: having good looks, pretty (≠ plain)
excites: provokes, stimulates □ **sudden:** all of a sudden
at first sight: on seeing her for the first time (love at...)
teeth (treated by dentists) □ **even:** uniform inquality, equal
for...purpose (use, need, objective), for eating
talkative: fond of talking □ **since:** because □ **inclined:** disposed,
wishing, willing □ **I was prepared to...:** I was ready to...
startled: shocked □ **bill of fare:** menu □ **for:** because
a great deal higher: much higher, a lot higher; a good deal of, a
large quantity of

generously: showing he was prepared to treat her to a good
expensive meal □ **far** too much, much too much; far too busy
nowadays: these days □ **fish(es)** live in water □ **I wonder if:**
wonder, ask oneself (if, whether..., who, what..., about (sth.)...)
early (in the year, in the season...): ≠ late
waiter: man who serves food at the tables in a restaurant; a waiter
(or waitress if it is a woman) waits *on* you
ordered it: asked the waiter to bring it □ **guest:** (sb.) you invite
hace: have (sth.) to eat or drink □ **while:** during the time that
cooked: prepared; cook, prepare food; cook, person who cooks
food □ **unless:** except if □ **I never mind caviare:** I never have
any objection to...; mind (sth.), object to (sth.), be opposed to (sth.)
my heart...: I nearly had a heart attack □ **afford:** be able to pay
for (caviare was "beyond his means")
by all means: certainly □ **chose:** selected □ **cheap(est):** inexpensive
chop: mutton chop, pork shop
you are unwise...: you shouldn't eat...; unwise, foolish, silly, stupid
expect...: think you'll work □ **heavy:** difficult to digest
I don't believe...: I don't think we should **overload**... (fill our
stomachs with too much food, with too heavy things)

"I never drink anything for luncheon," she said.

"Neither do I," I answered promptly.

"Except white wine," she proceeded as though I had not spoken. "These French white wines are so light. They're wonderful for the digestion."

"What would you like?" I asked, hospitable still, but not exactly effusive.

She gave me a bright and amicable flash of her white teeth.

10 "My doctor won't let me drink anything but champagne."

I fancy I turned a trifle pale. I ordered half a bottle. I mentioned casually that my doctor had absolutely forbidden me to drink champagne.

"What are you going to drink, then?"

"Water."

She ate the caviare and she ate the salmon. She talked gaily of art and literature and music. But I wondered what the bill would come to. When my mutton chop arrived she
20 took me quite seriously to task.

"I see that you're in the habit of eating a heavy luncheon. I'm sure it's a mistake. Why don't you follow my example and just eat one thing? I'm sure you'd feel ever so much better for it."

"I *am* only going to eat one thing," I said as the waiter came again with the bill of fare.

She waved him aside with an airy gesture.

"No, no, I never eat anything for luncheon. Just a bite, I never want more than that, and I eat that more as an
30 excuse for conversation than anything else. I couldn't possibly eat anything more—unless they had some of those giant asparagus. I should be sorry to leave Paris without

120

drink: drink, drank, drunk; have a drink

neither do: I don't drink either □ **promptly:** immediately

proceeded: continued, went on speaking □ **as though:** as if

light: (≠ heavy) easy to digest

wonderful: marvellous; the seven wonders of the world

hospitable: showing the wish to give attention to her needs

effusive: demonstrative, (too) enthusiastic, exuberant

she gave...bright (shining gaily) **amicable** (friendly) **flash...:** she smiled at me showing her teeth in a flash (*en un éclair*)

won't let me (allow me to) drink anything **but** (except) champagne: won't (not the future!) indicates it's always like that

fancy: imagine □ **turned:** became, went □ **a trifle:** a little...

casually: in passing, in a detached manner □ **forbidden:** ordered me not to (drink...); forbid, forbade, forbidden ≠ allow, permit; smoking is strictly forbidden; forbidden fruit

art: painting, sculpture...: arts faculty ≠ science faculty

come to: add up to, amount to; the bill came to £ 100

took me to task: spoke severely to me, blamed me, scolded me

habit: regular practice; be in the habit of + ing; habitual

mistake: error □ **follow** or take my example (a not e!)

one: just one; my one and only brother □ **ever so much better** is stronger than "so much" □ **for it:** if you ate only one thing

I *am*: (italics for emphasis) in actual fact I am going to eat one thing (but for another reason!...)

waved him aside, asked him to go with a wave, a gesture □ **airy:** casual, detached, with a little arrogance □ **a bite:** a little (sth.) to eat; I won't have a proper lunch, I'll just have a bite; bite, bit, bitten, cut (food) with the teeth □ **I couldn't possibly eat:** emphatic for "I couldn't eat..."

giant: very big; a giant □ **asparagus** (no plural!) are vegetables

having some of them."

My heart sank. I had seen them in the shops and I knew that they were horribly expensive. My mouth had often watered at the sight of them.

"Madame wants to know if you have any of those giant asparagus," I asked the waiter.

I tried with all my might to will him to say no. A happy smile spread over his broad, priest-like face, and he assured me that they had some so large, so splendid, so tender, that
10 it was a marvel.

"I'm not in the least hungry," my guest sighed, "but if you insist I don't mind having some asparagus."

I ordered them.

"Aren't you going to have any?"

"No, I never eat asparagus."

"I know there are people who don't like them. The fact is, you ruin your palate by all the meat you eat."

We waited for the asparagus to be cooked. Panic seized me. It was not a question now how much money I should
20 have left over for the rest of the month, but whether I had enough to pay the bill. It would be mortifying to find myself ten francs short and be obliged to borrow from my guest. I could not bring myself to do that. I knew exactly how much I had and if the bill came to more I made up my mind that I would put my hand in my pocket and with a dramatic cry start up and say it had been picked. Of course it would be awkward if she had not money enough either to pay the bill. Then the only thing would be to leave my watch and say I would come back and pay
30 later.

The asparagus appeared. They were enormous, succulent and appetising. The smell of the melted butter tickled

in the shops, probably in the shop-windows
my mouth had watered (had filled with water) on seeing them
at the sight of them (p. 116 l. 1) as they were so "appetising"
madame wants to know...: don't forget "to" after want
I asked the waiter: no preposition!
tried: did my best □ **might:** power, force □ **to will:** to force
a smile spread (extended) **over his broad priest-like face** (like a
priest's, a clergyman's): smile, happy expression; broad, wide,
large across □ **marvel:** wonder; marvellous, wonderful
not in the least: not at all □ **sighed:** gave a sigh (*soupir*)
I don't mind having asparagus: this negative way of saying
it is an understatement; in fact it means that she would love
to have asparagus; mind + ing, object to + ing; would you mind
shutting the window?

ruin: damage □ **palate:** *palais* □ **meat:** parts of animals used as food
panic seized me: panic took control of me; to panic, to get into
panic, (fam.) to feel panicky
left: he had 80 francs left before lunch □ **whether:** if
bill: (Am. check): list of things bought and their price
ten francs short, less than I needed □ **borrow:** get (sth.) after
promising to return it □ **bring myself to:** resolve to, take it into my
head to □ **I made up my mind:** I took or made the decision

start up: jump (in horror) □ **picked:** stolen, robbed (pickpocket)
awkward: embarrassing (he would feel ill at ease)
either: he does not have any money, she does not have any either
or neither does she (p. 120 l. 2) □ **watch** (indicates time): what time
is it *by* your watch?

smell: odour □ **melted:** made liquid □ **tickled:** excited

my nostrils as the nostrils of Jehovah were tickled by the
burned offerings of the virtuous Semites. I watched the
abandoned woman thrust them down her throat in large
voluptuous mouthfuls and in my polite way I discoursed on
the condition of the drama in the Balkans. At last she
finished.

"Coffee?" I said.

"Yes, just an ice-cream and coffee," she answered.

I was past caring now, so I ordered coffee for myself and
10 an ice-cream and coffee for her.

"You know, there's one thing I thoroughly believe in",
she said, as she ate the ice-cream. "One should always get
up from a meal feeling one could eat a little more."

"Are you still hungry?" I asked faintly.

"Oh, no, I'm not hungry; you see, I don't eat
luncheon. I have a cup of coffee in the morning and then
dinner, but I never eat more than one thing for luncheon.
I was speaking for you."

"Oh, I see"

20   Then a terrible thing happened. While we were waiting
for the coffee, the head waiter, with an ingratiating smile on
his false face, came up to us bearing a large basket full of
huge peaches. They had the blush of an innocent girl; they
had the rich tone of an Italian landscape. But surely
peaches were not in season then? Lord knew what they
cost. I knew too—a little later, for my guest, going on with
her conversation, absentmindedly took one.

"You see, you've filled your stomach with a lot of
meat"—my one miserable little chop—"and you can't eat
30 any more. But I've just had a snack and I shall enjoy a
peach."

The bill came and when I paid it I found that I had only

124

nostril(s): hole or opening at the end of the nose (for air)
burned offerings, like animals offered to God (on a fire)
abandoned: ≠ virtuous □ **thrust:** push □ **throat:** passage in neck for
food □ **mouthful(s):** as much as mouth can hold □ **in my polite way**
(manner) I **discoursed** (talked) □ **at** (long) **last:** in the end, after a
long time
coffee?: will you have some (coffee)?
ice-cream: vanilla ice-cream, chocolate ice-cream...
I was past (beyond) **caring:** I was indifferent now, I didn't care any
more; care, be anxious about
thoroughly: totally, entirely □ **believe:** believe in God...

meal: breakfast, lunch, tea, dinner, supper are meals
hungry: be hungry, be thirsty (be!) □ **faintly:** in a faint (low, weak)
voice (his heart sank again probably!) (≠ loud, strong)
in the morning, in the afternoon, in the evening: in!
for luncheon: no article! what will you have for dinner...?

happened: took place, occurred □ **waiting for...:** wait *for* (sth.)
head waiter: headmaster... □ **ingratiating:** showing one wishes
to gain favour □ **false:** ≠ true □ **bearing:** carrying
huge: giant □ **peach**(es): round fruit □ **blush:** redness spreading
over the face □ **tone:** colour □ **landscape:** country scenery
in season: ≠ out of season □ **Lord knew:** God knew; Lord Jesus
cost: how much does it cost?; costly, expensive □ **for:** because
absentmindedly: not thinking of what she was doing; mind, intellect
filled with: make full; fill *with*; full *of*
miserable: very small, poor in quality; a few miserable shillings; a
miserable pension □ **snack:** light meal □ **enjoy:** like, get pleasure
from, take delight in; I enjoyed that meal
paid: pay, paid, paid; pay (sb. for sth.); pay (sb. sth.); pay attention

enough for a quite inadequate tip. Her eyes rested for an instant on the three francs I left for the waiter and I knew that she thought me mean. But when I walked out of the restaurant I had the whole month before me and not a penny in my pocket.

"Follow my example," she said as we shook hands, "and never eat more than one thing for luncheon."

"I'll do better than that," I retorted, "I'll eat nothing for dinner to-night."

10   "Humorist!" she cried gaily, jumping into a cab. "You're quite a humorist!"

But I have had my revenge at last. I do not believe that I am a vindictive man, but when the immortal gods take a hand in the matter it is pardonable to observe the result with complacency. Today she weighs twenty-one stone.

inadequate: insufficient □ **tip:** money given to waiters □ **rested:** fell on, were directed on; her eyes rested on me

she thought me mean: she thought I was mean; mean, ungenerous, stingy, (fam.) tight-fisted □ **whole:** entire, complete; the whole family; all the members of the family (careful!)

shook hands: she shook hands *with* him and went away; a handshake; shake, shook, shaken

retorted: answered, replied; a retort, an incisive reply □ **I'll eat nothing...** (not to follow her example!...)

humorist: one who has *a* sense of humour □ **jumping** (quickly stepping, walking into) a **cab**, a taxi-cab, a taxi

revenge: have one's revenge *on* (sb.); in (out of) revenge for

vindictive: revengeful, unforgiving □ **take a hand in the matter** (question): interfere, take part in

complacency: satisfaction □ **stone** = 6,35 kg (no s in that sense!); how much does the lady weigh then? What does she weigh? What is her wei*ght*?

Grammaire au fil des nouvelles

Traduisez les phrases suivantes inspirées du texte (le premier chiffre renvoie aux pages, les suivants aux lignes) :

Il y avait longtemps que je ne l'avais vue... *Il y a* des années que nous nous sommes rencontrés... *Il y avait* vingt ans que je vivais à Paris (116.3,6,11).

Je pourrais m'en tirer *assez* bien (116.30).

Je ne mange *jamais* rien pour *le* déjeuner (composés de **some, any, no**; emploi de l'article, 118.12).

Les gens mangent beaucoup trop (**too** modifiant un verbe, 118.15).

Un beau saumon venait d'arriver (passé immédiat, 118.19).

Le garçon demanda si elle prendrait quelque chose pendant qu'on préparait le saumon (forme passive progressive, 118.21,22).

"Je ne bois jamais rien au déjeuner". *"Moi non plus"* (120.1,2).

Mon docteur ne m'autorise à boire que du champagne (... c'est comme ça; **let** et **make** + ...; **some, any, no** et composés, 120.10).

Je commandai une demi-bouteille (place de **a, an,** 120.12).

Qu'est-ce que vous allez boire? (expression de l'intention, 120.15).

Vous avez *l'habitude* de prendre un gros déjeuner (120.21).

Je ne pourrais rien manger d'autre (quantité supplémentaire, 120.31).

Je n'ai rien contre le fait de prendre des asperges (**mind** + ... 122.12).

Nous attendîmes que les asperges fussent cuites (proposition infinitive introduite par **for**, 122.18).

Ce serait gênant si elle n'avait pas assez d'argent *non plus* (122.28).

Il y a une chose à laquelle je crois à fond... (suppression du relatif et rejet de la préposition, 124.11).

On devrait toujours se lever de table avec le sentiment qu'on *pourrait* en manger un peu plus (**one** avec un sens très général, universel; quantité supplémentaire, 124.12).

THE LETTER

by Bernard Malamud (1914-1986)

Bernard Malamud was born in Brooklyn and educated at the City College of New York and at Columbia University. After various odd jobs he began to teach in 1939. He started writing and publishing short stories in 1941. His remarkable first novel, *The Natural,* appeared in 1952, followed in 1957 by *The Assistant.* In addition to novels *(The Tenants...)* his later work includes collections of short stories, available in Penguin Books Ltd.: *The Magic Barrel, Idiots First* and *Rembrand's Hat* from which *The Letter* is taken. Some of Malamud's stories speak eloquently of the need to communicate. Others are full of bitter humour. All of them are characterised by a tragi-comic tone with grotesque, tender and poignant elements. *The Letter* illustrates these qualities very well.

At the gate stands Teddy holding his letter.

On Sunday afternoons Newman sat with his father on a white bench in the open ward. The son had brought a pineapple tart but the old man wouldn't eat it.

Twice during the two and a half hours he spent in the ward with his father, Newman said, "Do you want me to come back next Sunday or don't you? Do you want to have next Sunday off?"

10   The old man said nothing. Nothing meant yes or it meant no. If you pressed him to say which he wept.

"All right, I'll see you next Sunday. But if you want a week off some time, let me know. I want a Sunday off myself."

His father said nothing. Then his mouth moved and after a while he said, "Your mother didn't talk to me like that. She didn't like to leave any dead chickens in the bathtub. When is she coming to see me here?"

"Pa, she's been dead since before you got sick and tried 20 to take your life. Try to keep that in your memory."

"Don't ask me to believe that one," his father said, and Newman got up to go to the station where he took the Long Island Rail Road train to New York City.

He said, "Get better, Pa," when he left, and his father answered, "Don't tell me that. I am better."

Sundays after he left his father in Ward 12 of Building B and walked across the hospital grounds, that spring and dry summer, at the arched iron-barred gate between brick posts under a towering oak that shadowed the raw red brick wall, 30 he met Teddy standing there with his letter in his hand. Newman could have got out through the main entrance of Building B of the hospital complex, but this way

130

gate: outside door to hospital, park...; garden gate

on Sunday afternoons: every Sunday afternoon (no s!)
open ward: large room in hospital (≠ private room)
pineapple: *ananas* □ **wouldn't eat:** didn't want to
twice: once, twice, three times □ **two and *a* half hours**
do you want me to come: infinitive clause (want, expect...)
next: coming immediately after, in order, following
have... off: without me coming; have a day off (without work)
meant: mean, meant, meant, signify, indicate; meaning (of word)
pressed: insisted □ **which:** either yes or no □ **wept:** cried (shed tears;
tears poured from his eyes)
some time: one day or other; I'll take my holiday some time in July

mouth: don't talk with your mouth full □ **moved:** movement
a while: a (short) period of time; just wait for a while
leave things undone (she was meticulous) □ **chicken:** *poulet*
bathtub (Am.): bath; have a bath, to bath (wash in a bath)
Pa: father, dad □ **sick:** ill, unwell □ **tried:** attempted
take your life: commit suicide, kill yourself
believe: accept as true what (sb.) says; believe in God
got up: stood up (from the bench) □ **(railway) station**
rail road (Am.): railway
get better: be well, physically (or mentally...) in good form
I am better: my health is improving

grounds: land, gardens round building □ **dry:** ≠ wet, rainy
arched: curved □ **iron:** the most common metal □ **post:** pillar
towering: very tall □ **oak:** *chêne* □ **shadowed the raw brick...:** made
a shadow *(ombre)* on; raw, rough, unrefined
main entrance as opposed to back entrance, side entrance; main,
principal; main street

to the railroad station was shorter.   The gate was open to visitors on Sundays only.

Teddy was a stout soft man in loose grey institutional clothes and canvas slippers.   He was fifty or more and maybe so was his letter.   He held it as he always held it, as though he had held it always, a thick squarish finger-soiled blue envelope with unsealed flap.   Inside were four sheets of cream paper with nothing written on them.   After he had looked at the paper the first time, Newman had
10 handed the envelope back to Teddy, and the green-uniformed guard had let him out of the gate.   Sometimes there were other patients standing by the gate who wanted to walk out with Newman but the guard said they couldn't.

"What about mailing my letter," Teddy said on Sundays.

He handed Newman the finger-smudged envelope.   It was easier to take, then hand back, than to refuse to take it.

20   The mailbox hung on a short cement pole just outside the iron gate on the other side of the road, a few feet from the oak tree.   Teddy would throw a right jab in its direction as though at the mailbox through the gate.   Once it had been painted red and was now painted blue.   There was also a mailbox in the doctor's office in each ward, Newman had reminded him, but Teddy said he didn't want the doctor reading his letter.

"You bring it to the office and so they read it."

"That's his job", Newman answered.

30   "Not on my head," said Teddy.   "Why don't you mail it?   It won't do you any good if you don't."

"There's nothing in it to mail."

stout: corpulent □ **soft** ≠ firm □ **loose:** too big □ **institutional clothes:** uniform □ **canvas slippers:** light shoes with top made from canvas (cloth, soft material, also used for tents) generally worn indoors □ **squarish:** more or less square

finger-soiled: with dirty finger marks □ **with unsealed flap:** open, with flap of envelope not stuck down □ **sheets of cream** (coloured) **paper:** sheet, piece of paper

handed... back: given back; to hand (sb.) a book, to pass
green-uniformed: with a green uniform; long-haired, blue-eyed...
by: near; close by, hard by, very near
said: say (sth. to sb.); tell (sb. sth. or tell sth. to sb.)

what about mailing: what (how) about a drink...? (to make suggestions); to mail (Am.), to post; mailbox (Am.), letterbox
finger-smudged: (l. 11) finger-soiled (l. 7); smudge, dirty mark
easier: less embarrassing (Newman felt less uncomfortable)

hung: was fixed □ **pole:** post, pillar □ **outside:** ≠ inside
feet: 1 foot = 12 inches = 30,48 cm; 1 inch = 2,54 cm
would (usually) **throw a jab** (like a boxer with his right hand)
as though: as if □ **once:** some time ago, formerly
painted red... painted blue: no prepositions!
each ward: every single ward
reminded him: made him remember; remind me to phone Lily
the doctor reading...: the fact that the doctor read...
so: in consequence, consequently, therefore
his job: his work, his duty, his business
not on my head: certainly not! He won't read mine!
it won't do you any good: nothing good will happen to you, some misfortune will happen to you; do (sb.) good ≠ do (sb.) harm

133

"That's what you say."

His heavy head was set on a short sunburned neck, the coarse grizzled hair cropped an inch from the skull. One of his eyes was a fleshy grey, the other was wall-eyed. He stared beyond Newman when he talked to him, sometimes through his shoulder. And Newman noticed he never so much as glanced at the blue envelope when it was momentarily out of his hand, when Newman was holding it. Once in a while he pointed a short finger at something
10 but said nothing. When he said nothing he rose a little on the balls of his toes. The guard did not interfere when Teddy handed Newman the letter every Sunday.

Newman gave it back.

"It's your mistake," said Teddy. Then he said, "I got my walking privileges. I'm almost sane. I fought in Guadalcanal."

Newman said he knew that.

"Where did you fight?"

"Nowhere yet."
20 "Why don't you mail my letter out?"

"It's for your own good the doctor reads it."

"That's a hot one." Teddy stared at the mailbox through Newman's shoulder.

"The letter isn't addressed to anybody and there's no stamp on it."

"Put one on. They won't let me buy one three or three ones."

"It's eight cents now. I'll put one on if you address the envelope."
30 "Not me," said Teddy.

Newman no longer asked why.

"It's not that kind of a letter."

134

that's what you say (but you are wrong...)

heavy: big □ **set:** placed □ **sunburned:** brown □ **neck:** *cou*

coarse: ≠ fine □ **grizzled:** greyish □ **cropped:** cut □ **skull:** *crâne*

fleshy: flesh, *chair* □ **wall-eyed:** with lots of white

stared: looked fixedly □ **beyond:** farther than

shoulder: *épaule* □ **noticed** (saw, realized) **he never so much as** (he did not even) **glanced at** (looked at)...; glance, give a rapid look; a glance, a quick look

once in a while: sometimes, not often; while, space of time

rose: went up (higher); rise, rose risen

on the balls of his toes: *sur la pointe des pieds* □ **interfere** (with other people's business)

you are making a **mistake** (error) □ **I got** (Am.) = I have

I may **walk** where I want □ **almost:** nearly □ **sane:** ≠ mad

Guadalcanal: Pacific island where intense fighting took place between the Japanese and the Americans in World War II

fight: fight, fought, fought

nowhere yet: I did not fight anywhere yet (not as yet!)

for your own (personal) **good** (benefit); do (sb.) good (p. 132 l. 31)

that's a hot one: that's a very good one, a very good joke (sth. said or done to make other people laugh)

stamp: don't forget to stick a stamp on the envelope!

one three (cent) stamp; there are 100 cents in one dollar

three ones: three one cent stamps

it's eight cents: the postage is eight cents (postage: cost of sending a letter or parcel by post)

not me: certainly not; address an envelope, write an address on...

Newman no longer asked: Newman stopped, gave up asking why

that kind of a letter: or that kind (sort) of letter

He asked what kind it was.

"Blue with white paper inside of it."

"Saying what?"

"Shame on you," said Teddy.

Newman left on the four o'clock train. The ride home was not so bad as the ride there, though Sundays were murderous.

Teddy holds his letter.

"No luck?"

10   "No luck," said Newman.

"It's off your noodle."

He handed the envelope to Newman anyway and after a while Newman gave it back.

Teddy stared at his shoulder.

Ralph holds the finger-soiled blue envelope.

20   On Sunday a tall lean grim old man, clean-shaven, faded-eyed, wearing a worn-thin World War I overseas cap on his yellowed white head, stood at the gate with Teddy. He looked eighty.

The guard in the green uniform told him to step back, he was blocking the gate.

"Step back, Ralph, you're in the way of the gate."

"Why don't you stick it in the box on your way out?" Ralph asked in a gravelly old man's voice, handing the letter to Newman.

30   Newman wouldn't take it. "Who are you?"

Teddy and Ralph said nothing.

"It's his father," the guard at the gate said.

he asked what kind it was: "what kind was it?" he asked
inside of it (Am.): inside it, in it

shame on you: you ought to be ashamed; shame, humiliation
ride: journey (on the train, on the bus..., on horseback)
the ride there: to the hospital; it takes an hour there and back
murderous: terrible, infernal, unbearable (because there were too
many people on the trains)
luck: good fortune; I wish you luck in your exams
no luck: or hard luck; be lucky ≠ be unlucky
it's off your noodle: it's mad, crazy; noodle (fam.), head
anyway: in any case, at any rate

hold: hold, held, held □ **envelope:** only one p!

lean: ≠ fat □ **grim:** severe □ **clean-shaven:** *bien rasé* □ **faded:** pale,
dull □ **worn-thin... overseas cap** *(calot)*: made thin by continued use;
wear (clothes), wore, worn □ **yellowed:** turned yellow (like paper
with age) □ **looked:** gave the impression of being...
to step: walk; step, movement of foot in walking
blocking: make movement difficult or impossible by putting (sth.)
or getting □ **in the way** of; get out of my way!
stick: (fam.) put □ **on your way out:** as you go out
gravelly: rough, hard and unpleasant, grating (≠ smooth); in a
gravelly old man's voice (notice the preposition "in" and the
meaning of the genitive with "a" or "an": a voice typical of old
men in general)

"Whose?"

"Teddy."

"My God," said Newman.   "Are they both in here?"

"That's right," said the guard.

"Was he just admitted or has he been here all the while?"

"He just got his walking privileges returned again.   They were revoked about a year."

"I got them back after five years," Ralph said.

10   "One year."

"Five."

"It's astonishing anyway," Newman said.   "Neither one of you resembles the other."

"Who do you resemble?" asked Ralph.

Newman couldn't say.

"What war were you in?" Ralph asked.

"No war at all."

"That settles your pickle.   Why don't you mail my letter?"

20   Teddy stood by sullenly.   He rose on his toes and threw a short right and left at the mailbox.

"I thought it was Teddy's letter."

"He told me to mail it for him.   He fought at Iwo Jima.   We fought two wars.   I fought in the Marne and the Argonne Forest.   I had both my lungs gassed with mustard gas.   The wind changed and the Huns were gassed.   That's not all that were."

"Tough turd," said Teddy.

"Mail it anyway for the poor kid," said Ralph.   His tall
30 body trembled.   He was an angular man with deep-set bluish eyes and craggy features that looked as though they had been hacked out of a tree.

whose: or "whose father?"

Teddy: it should be "Teddy's" (father)

are they both?...: they are both here, both of them are here

that's right: or exact, correct (≠ wrong)

admitted: be admitted to hospital (allowed to enter, let in)

all the while: all the time

returned: given back

about: approximately, roughly

astonishing: surprising, amazing, astounding □ **neither:** neither is English; both of them are American (careful!) □ **resemble:** resemble (sb.) (no preposition!), look like (sb.)

what war were you in?: notice the position of "in"; what are you looking *at*? Who were you talking *to*?

that settles (solves) **your pickle** (difficult situation)

sullenly: sullen: morose, ill-humoured (≠ cheerful, jovial)

a short right and left (like a boxer again): jab (p. 132 l. 22)

I thought: think, thought, thought

Iwo Jima: Pacific island, the scene of fierce fighting in 1945

war: World War I or the Great War, World War II

both my lungs (breathing organs): note position of "both"

mustard gas: *gaz moutarde* □ **Huns:** (pejorative) Germans

that was not all that were: they were not the only ones who...

tough turd; so what!; tough, hard; turd (slang) shit, piece of excrement □ **kid:** (fam.) child

angular: thin, lean □ **deep-set:** *enfoncé dans l'orbite*

craggy: rough in appearance □ **features:** parts of the face

hacked: cut roughly, chop; hack down a tree (with an axe)

"I told your son I would if he wrote something on the paper," Newman said.

"What do you want it to say?"

"Anything he wants it to. Isn't there somebody he wants to communicate with? If he doesn't want to write it he could tell me what to say and I'll write it out."

"Tough turd," said Teddy.

"He wants to communicate to me," said Ralph.

"It's not a bad idea," Newman said. "Why doesn't he
10 write a few words to you? Or you could write a few words to him."

"A Bronx cheer on you."

"It's my letter," Teddy said.

"I don't care who writes it," said Newman. "I could write a message for you wishing him luck. I could say you hope he gets out of here soon."

"A Bronx cheer to that."

"Not in my letter," Teddy said.

"Not in mine either," said Ralph grimly. "Why don't
20 you mail it like it is? I bet you're afraid to."

"No I'm not."

"I'll bet you are."

"No I'm not."

"I have my bets going."

"There's nothing to mail. There's nothing in the letter. It's a blank."

"What makes you think so?" asked Ralph. "There's a whole letter in there. Plenty of news."

"I'd better be going," Newman said, "or I'll miss my
30 train."

The guard opened the gate to let him out. Then he shut the gate.

140

I told your son I would (mail it); son, male child
paper: notepaper, paper for (private) correspondence

anything he wants it to (say): anything (everything) he wants the letter to say (infinitive with want, expect, prefer, (would) like, (would) love: Teddy would like him to mail his letter; they expected us to come later (notice the personal pronouns) (p. 130 l. 7)

a few words: a few, many + countable nouns (a few pieces of bread); a little, much + uncountable nouns (much bread)
a Bronx-cheer: (slang) a loud noise made in derision, imitative of a fart *(pet)*
I don't care: care, be anxious, worried or concerned about; I don't care what happens; I couldn't care less
hope: expect and desire; hopeful ☐ **soon:** in a short time; as soon as possible; the sooner the better; you'll have to do it sooner or later

grimly: severely, sternly, without mercy: grim (p. 136 l. 20)
like it is: as it is ☐ **I bet you are afraid to** (mail it): I'm certain...; bet, bet or betted, bet or betted, risk money on a (horse) race, game...; make a bet

I have my bets going: I'm still ready to bet you are afraid (I persist in thinking you are afraid, I maintain you are...)
it's a blank: there's nothing written in it; a blank, an empty space; a blank cheque... (blank is an adjective too)
whole: entire ☐ **plenty of news:** a lot of information
I had better indicates obligation ☐ **I'll miss my train,** I won't get it; miss, fail to get; miss the point (of a joke...) (in order)
to let him (walk, step) ☐ **out:** let (sb.) out ≠ let (sb.) in

Teddy turned away and stared over the oak tree into the summer sun with his grey eye and his wall-eyed one.

Ralph trembled at the gate.

"Who do you come here to see on Sundays?" he called to Newman.

"My father."

"What war was he in?"

"The war in his head."

"Has he got his walking privileges?"

10   "No, they won't give him any."

"What I mean, he's crazy?"

"That's right," said Newman, walking away.

"So are you," said Ralph.   "Why don't you come back in here and hang around with the rest of us?"

turned away (in another direction) □ **over:** ≠ under
one is used to avoid the repetition of "eye"
trembled: tremble or shake (with cold, excitement...)
he called to Newman: he said to Newman in a loud voice; call, shout, cry

what war was he in? see place of preposition (p. 138 l. 16)
the war in his head: the war he is obsessed with

mean: want to say; mean, meant, meant □ **he's crazy:** or (slang) he's off his "noodle", off his rocker, round the bend
so are you: you are mad too; he smokes, so do I
hang around: hang about, stay there (doing nothing definite)

Grammaire au fil des nouvelles

Traduisez les phrases suivantes inspirées du texte (le premier chiffre renvoie aux pages, les suivants aux lignes) :

Veux-tu que je revienne dimanche prochain ou non ? (proposition infinitive ; question tag, 130.7,8).

Si vous le pressiez pour dire l'un ou l'autre (oui ou non), il pleurait (notion de choix, 130.11).

Ne me demande pas de croire celle-là. Ne me dis pas ça (impératif négatif 2e personne, 130.21,25).

Newman *aurait pu* sortir par l'entrée principale (130.31).

Il y avait d'*autres* patients debout près du portail *qui* voulaient sortir avec Newman (132.12).

Pourquoi ne postes-tu pas ma lettre ? (forme interro-négative, 134.20).

La lettre n'est adressée à personne et il n'y a pas de timbre dessus (**some, any, no**, 134.24).

Ils ne me laissent pas acheter de timbres (**let** et **make** + ... 134.26).

Sont-ils tous les deux ici ?... J'ai eu les deux poumons gazés (**both**, 138.3,25).

Est-il ici depuis toujours ? (138.5).

Que veux-tu qu'elle dise ? (la lettre) (proposition infinitive, 140.3).

Il veut communiquer avec moi (**want, like, prefer** ne sont pas suivis de la simple base verticale, 140.8).

Pourrais-tu lui écrire *quelques* mots ? (140.10).

Qu'est-ce qui te fait croire cela ? (**make** et **let** + ... 140.27).

Je ferais mieux de m'en aller (**had better** et **had rather** + ... 140.29).

Ce que je veux dire... il est fou ?... *Toi aussi* (142.11,13).

A NIGHT AT A COTTAGE

by Richard Hughes (1900-1976)

Richard Hughes was educated at Charterhouse and Oriel College, Oxford. He started his career as a playwright with *The Sister's Tragedy* (1942) which is said to have been praised by Bernard Shaw as "the finest one-act play ever written". A contributor to London and American literary journals, he has also published poems, short stories and children's books *(Don't blame me, The Spider's Palace, Gertrude's Child, Gertrude and the Mermaid)*. His greatest success was with two novels : *A High Wind in Jamaica* (1929) (title of the American edition: *The Innocent Voyage*) and *In Hazard* (1938).

In *A Night at a Cottage* the author excels in creating an atmosphere of fear and horror...

On the evening that I am considering I passed by some ten or twenty cosy barns and sheds without finding one to my liking for Worcestershire lanes are devious and muddy, and it was nearly dark when I found an empty cottage set back from the road in a little bedraggled garden. There had been heavy rain earlier in the day, and the straggling fruit-trees still wept over it.

But the roof looked sound, there seemed no reason why it should not be fairly dry inside—as dry, at any rate, as I
10 was likely to find anywhere.

I decided and with a long look up the road, and a long look down the road, I drew an iron bar from the lining of my coat and forced the door, which was only held by a padlock and two staples. Inside, the darkness was damp and heavy. I struck a match, and with its haloed light I saw the black mouth of a passage somewhere ahead of me and then it spluttered out. So I closed the door carefully, though I had little reason to fear passers-by at such a dismal hour in so remote a lane and lighting another match, I crept
20 down this passage to a little room at the far end, where the air was a bit clearer, for all that the window was boarded across. Moreover, there was a little rusted stove in this room and thinking it too dark for any to see the smoke, I ripped up part of the wainscot with my knife, and soon was boiling my tea over a bright, small fire, and drying some of the day's rain out of my steamy clothes. Presently I piled the stove with wood to its top bar, and setting my boots where they would best dry, I stretched my body out to sleep.

30 I cannot have slept very long, for when I woke the fire was still burning brightly. It is not easy to sleep for long together on the level boards of a floor, for the limbs grow

by: near; a passer-by (l. 18) □ **some ten...:** about ten
cosy: comfortable □ **barns, sheds:** buildings for grain, animals...
...liking: I liked □ **lane(s):** country road □ **devious:** ≠ straight □
muddy: *boueux* □ **empty:** with nobody in it □ **cottage set back...:**
small house a little away from... □ **bedraggled:** wet (with rain) and
dirty □ **heavy** ≠ light □ **earlier** ≠ later □ **straggling:** irregular,
disorderly □ **wept:** cried (with drops of rain falling from them)
roof: top covering of house □ **sound:** in good condition
fairly: quite □ **dry** ≠ wet □ **at any rate:** in any case
as I was likely: as I stood a chance of finding anywhere else
with a long look...: after examining the road (right and left)
drew: took out; draw, drew, drawn □ **lining:** *doublure*

padlock: *cadenas* □ **staple(s):** *crampon* □ **damp:** wet
struck a match (like for lighting a cigarette) □ **haloed:** with a halo
round it □ **mouth:** entrance □ **ahead of:** in front of
spluttered out: went out (hesitantly) □ **closed:** shut □ **carefully:** with
attention □ **fear:** be afraid of □ **dismal:** sinister
remote: isolated □ **lighting:** striking □ **crept:** walked furtively
the far end: the other end (further away)
a bit: a little □ **for all...:** although □ **boarded:** covered with boards,
planks □ **moreover:** in addition □ **rusted stove:** stove (*poêle*)
corroded by rust □ **any**(body) □ **smoke** (from chimney)
ripped up: cut off, tore off □ **wainscot:** wooden panelling (*boiserie*)
(shining) **bright:** nice and bright □ **drying:** to dry, make dry
steamy: wet; steam (*vapeur*) □ **presently:** very soon □ **piled...:**
filled it as much as possible □ **setting:** putting □ **boot(s):**
heavy shoes □ **dry:** get dry □ **stretched my body out:** lay down;
stretch, extend
for: because □ **woke:** stopped sleeping
for long together: for a long time without interruption
level: horizontal □ **floor:** *parquet* □ **limbs:** arms and legs □ **grow,**

numb, and any movement wakes. I turned over, and was about to go again to sleep when I was startled to hear steps in the passage. As I have said, the window was boarded, and there was no other door from the little room—no cupboard even—in which to hide. It occurred to me rather grimly that there was nothing to do but to sit up and face the music, and that would probably mean being haled back to Worcester jail, which I had left two bare days before, and where, for various reasons, I had no anxiety to
10 be seen again.

The stranger did not hurry himself, but presently walked slowly down the passage, attracted by the light of the fire and when he came in he did not seem to notice me where I lay huddled in a corner, but walked straight over to the stove and warmed his hands at it. He was dripping wet, wetter than I should have thought it possible for a man to get, even on such a rainy night and his clothes were old and worn. The water dripped from him on to the floor; he wore no hat, and the straight hair over his eyes dripped
20 water that sizzled spitefully on the embers.

It occurred to me at once that he was no lawful citizen, but another wanderer like myself; a gentleman of the Road; so I gave him some sort of greeting, and we were presently in conversation. He complained much of the cold and the wet, and huddled himself over the fire, his teeth chattering and his face an ill white.

'No,' I said, 'it is no decent weather for the Road, this. But I wonder this cottage isn't more frequented, for it's a tidy little bit of a cottage.'
30 Outside the pale dead sunflowers and giant weeds stirred in the rain.

'Time was,' he answered, 'there wasn't a tighter little cot

148

get + adjective: become □ **numb** (with cold...): unable to feel
startled: taken by surprise □ **(foot) step(s):** sound made by the
movement of the foot in walking

cupboard (for dishes, clothes) □ **it occurred to me:** the idea came
to my mind □ **grimly:** horribly □ **but** (except) **to sit up** (from a lying
position) ...**face the music** (difficulty) □ **haled:** taken by force
jail: prison □ **two bare days:** not more than two days; barely, hardly
anxiety: strong desire; I am anxious to go on holiday

stranger: (sb.) you don't know □ **hurry:** move or do (sth.) quickly
or excitedly
notice: pay attention to, see
huddled: with limbs drawn close to body □ **straight:** directly
warmed: made warm □ **dripping wet:** so wet that rain dripped (fell
in drops) from his clothes
even: even a child knows that; even if, even though
worn: in a bad condition from being used too long
wore: wear (clothes), wore, worn □ **straight:** ≠ curved
sizzled: *grésillait* □ **spitefully** ≠ kindly □ **embers:** wood burning in
dying fire □ **lawful** (legal): ... that he was a criminal
wanderer: vagabond, tramp, vagrant, "gentleman of the Road"
greeting: message of welcome like "Good evening", "Hello"...
complained...: said that he suffered from the cold
his teeth chattering (trembling, shaking from cold); a tooth
an ill white: white as if he was ill or sick

I wonder: I'm surprised...
tidy: in good order, clean, neat, nice and clean
sunflower(s): *tournesol* □ **giant weeds stirred:** tall unwanted wild
plants (which prevent others from growing) moved...
there was a time when □ **tight(er):** nice, clean, in good order

in the co-anty, nor a purtier garden. A regular little parlour, she was. But now no folk'll live in it, and there's very few tramps will stop here either.'

There were none of the rags and tins and broken food about that you find in a place where many beggars are used to stay.

'Why's that?' I asked.

He gave a very troubled sigh before answering.

'Gho-asts,' he said, 'gho-asts. Him that lived here. It
10 is a mighty sad tale, and I'll not tell it you but the upshot of it was that he drowned himself, down to the mill-pond. All slimy, he was, and floating, when they pulled him out of it. There are fo-aks have seen un floating on the pond, and fo-aks have seen un set round the corner of the school, waiting for his childer. Seems as if he had forgotten, like, how they were all gone dead, and the why he drowned hisself. But there are some say he walks up and down this cottage, up and down; like when the small-pox had' em, and they couldn't sleep but if they heard his
20 feet going up and down by their do-ars. Drowned hisself down to the pond, he did and now he Walks.'

The stranger sighed again, and I could hear the water squelch in his boots as he moved himself.

'But it doesn't do for the likes of us to get superstitious,' I answered. 'It wouldn't do for us to get seeing ghosts, or many's the wet night we'd be lying in the roadway.'

'No,' he said; 'no, it wouldn't do at all. I never had belief in Walks myself.'

I laughed.

30 'Nor I that,' I said. 'I never see ghosts, whoever may.'

He looked at me again in his queer melancholy fashion.

co-anty: country □ **purtier:** prettier □ **regular:** real
parlour: (nice cosy) sitting-room □ **folk(s):** people
(who) will (as a rule, usually) **stop...** (stop at a hotel)
rags: old torn clothes □ (*sardine...*) **tin(s)** □ **broken food about:**
uneaten pieces of bread... here and there □ **beggar(s):** one who lives
by begging (asking for money, food, clothes...); notice the strange
incorrect language of the "stranger"
troubled: anxious, worried □ **sigh:** *soupir*; give a sigh, to sigh
gho-ast(s): ghost, phantom □ **him that lived:** he who lived
mighty: very □ **tale:** story □ **the upshot:** the result, the end
drowned himself: killed himself in the water of the **mill-pond** (small
lake by the mill, *moulin*) □ **slimy:** full of mud, slime
fo-aks (folks who have seen) **un**(him)
set: standing
childer: children (one child!) □ (it) **seems as if**
like: so to say, so it seems □ **the** (reason) **why...**
some (people who) **say he walks...** (he haunts this cottage)
small-pox: serious infectious disease (*variole*)
but if: except if
do-ar(s): door
he walks: he comes back as a ghost (haunting the house)
sighed: to sigh, to give a sigh, to heave a sigh (l. 8)
squelch: make sound of liquid (pressed by feet inside shoes)
it doesn't do (it's against our interests) for **the likes of us** (for people
like us) □ **get** (start, develop the habit of seeing...)
many's the wet (rainy) **night:** we would spend many nights...

belief in the existence of ghosts; religious beliefs; believe in God
laughed: (sth.) amusing makes you laugh; laughter (noun)
nor...: I don't believe in that either □ **whoever may:** even if others
may see... □ **queer:** strange, odd □ **melancholy:** sad
fashion: manner, way

'No,' he said. ''Spect you don't ever. Some folk
doan't. It's hard enough for poor fellows to have no
money to their lodging, apart from gho-asts sceering
them.'

'It's the coppers, not spooks, make me sleep uneasy,' said
I. 'What with coppers, and meddlesome-minded folk, it
isn't easy to get a night's rest nowadays.'

The water was still oozing from his clothes all about the
floor, and a dank smell went up from him.

10 'God! man,' I cried, 'can't you *never* get dry?'

'Dry?' He made a little coughing laughter. 'Dry? I
shan't never be dry... 'tisn't the likes of us that ever get dry,
be it wet *or* fine, winter *or* summer. See that!'

He thrust his muddy hands up to the wrist in the fire,
glowering over it fiercely and madly. But I caught up my
two boots and ran crying out into the night.

spect...: I expect (suppose) you never see ghosts ("walks")
doan't: don't □ **hard:** difficult □ **fellows:** people, men
to (pay for) **their lodging** (place to stay in) □ **apart from...:** to say
nothing of... **sceering** (scaring them, making them afraid)
coppers (policemen), not **spooks** (ghosts) who disturb my **sleep**
what with one thing and another □ **meddlesome:** interfering with
other people's business □ **rest:** break □ **nowadays:** these days
oozing: passing slowly through, flowing out gradually
dank: unpleasantly wet and cold □ **a smell:** smell, smelt, smellt
man (used when one is excited): hurry up, man!   Wake up, man!
coughing: smoke, a bald cold makes you cough
shan't: shall not □ **'tisn't...:** people like us never get dry...
be it wet...: in wet or **fine** (sunny) weather just the same
thrust: pushed suddenly □ **wrist** joins hand and arm
glowering, looking in a **fierce,** angry way, like a madman □ **I caught
up,** I picked up... □ **crying:** shouting, yelling □ ran **out**

Grammaire au fil des nouvelles

Traduisez les phrases suivantes inspirées du texte (le premier chiffre renvoie aux pages, les suivants aux lignes) :

Je passai près de quelque dix ou vingt granges sans en trouver une seule à mon goût (prépositions suivies du gérondif, 146.1,2).

Il y avait eu de la grosse pluie plus tôt dans la journée (146.5).

J'avais *peu de* raisons de craindre des passants à une heure si lugubre dans un chemin *aussi* retiré (place de **a, an, such** et **so**, 146.18,19).

Il faisait trop sombre pour que quelqu'un voie la fumée (proposition infinitive introduite par **for**, 146.23).

Les membres s'engourdissent et tout mouvement (*n'importe quel* mouvement) réveille (148.1).

Il n'y avait pas de placard où se cacher (relatif, 148.5)

Cela voudrait probablement dire être ramené de force dans la prison de Worcester que j'avais quittée à peine deux jours auparavant (gérondif, 148.7 ; relatif, 148.8).

Il ne portait pas de chapeau (**some, any, no**, 148.19).

Personne n'y *habite*, peu de vagabonds s'y *arrêtent* (c'est comme ça maintenant, 150.2,3).

Il poussa un soupir avant de répondre (prépositions suivies du gérondif, 150.8).

Il s'est noyé (volontairement) (pronoms réfléchis, 150.11).

J'entendais l'eau faire flic flac dans ses gros souliers (verbes de perception + ..., 150.23).

Ça ne ferait pas notre affaire que de commencer à voir des fantômes (proposition infinitive introduite par **for**, 150.25).

C'est assez dur pour de pauvres types de n'avoir pas d'argent pour leur logement (place de **enough**, 152.2).

Ce n'est pas facile d'avoir *une nuit de sommeil* par les temps qui courent (génitif pour exprimer la durée ou la distance, 152.7).

CHARITY

by Liam O'Flaherty (1896-1984)

Liam O'Flaherty was born, as he himself said, on "a storm-beaten rock", that is on Inishmore, the largest of the Aran Islands. He was educated at University College, Dublin. He fought with the Irish Guards during the First World War and took part in the Irish Revolution. His major works include *Famine,* a historical novel, *The Informer, Insurrection, Shame the Devil,* an autobiography (including a beautiful story, *The Caress*) and numerous short stories, fifty-three of which are published in two volumes by New English Library Ltd. In his stories which are often very short, the Irish writer describes in evocative lyrical prose the land and the people he loves so much.

The parish priest was in his library, lolling in a chair by the window with his coat off. It was a dreadfully hot day and he had had a tough morning, visiting sick in an outlying part of his parish. He was counting on half an hour's rest before dinner when suddenly a timid and prolonged knock came to the door.

'Come in,' said the parish priest wearily, sitting up and reaching for his coat.

Nicholas Reddon, an ex-schoolmaster and a notorious
10 drunkard, slouched into the room. He had an extraordinary appearance, pathetic, yet contemptible and repulsive. His once handsome, slim figure was clothed in an assortment of shabby garments that looked still more shabby because they tried to be genteel. His long, thin, intelligent face was mournful, blotched and hardened by a fixed expression of defiant arrogance. His eyes were bloodshot and blinked continually.

He peered around the room suspiciously. Then he entered, closed the door quietly and made a slight bow,
20 scraping his right foot. He stood facing the priest, twirling his cap on his right forefinger.

'Father Waters,' he said, 'I came to see you on a small matter. You will pardon the interruption when I—'

'Sit down,' said the parish priest, wrinkling his forehead and buttoning his coat.

The ex-schoolmaster sat down on the edge of a chair and placed his cap and his two hands between his knees.

'You've been drinking,' said the priest sharply.

'Father Waters—'

30 'You needn't deny it, Mr. Reddon,' continued the priest, 'and I know what the small matter is.'

The priest stood up abruptly and waved his arms. He

156

parish: part of diocese □ **priest:** clergyman □ **lolling** prostrate... **by** (near)... □ **off:** ≠ on □ **dreadfully:** very

tough: hard, tiring □ **sick:** ill □ **outlying:** far from centre

counting on, expecting to have a **rest,** a break, some sleep

suddenly: all of a sudden □ **knock** (noun): also to knock; please knock on (at) the door before entering

wearily: weary, very tired, exhausted

reaching (his hand) **for his coat** in order to pick it up

notorious: (pejorative) unfavourably known

drunkard: alcoholic □ **slouched:** walked in a lazy tired way

contemptible: ≠ admirable, honourable; contempt, disdain

once: in the past □ **handsome, slim figure... clothed:** attractive, nicely thin body...dressed □ **shabby garments:** worn old clothes

genteel: chic, imitating upper social classes

mournful: ≠ joyful □ **blotched:** with dirty marks □ **hardened:** made hard, severe, stern □ **defiant:** rebellious (≠ submissive)

bloodshot: red like blood □ **blinked:** shut and opened quickly

peered: scrutinized □ **suspiciously:** with suspicion

quietly: ≠ noisily □ **...slight bow:** (salutation) bent his head a little

scraping and bowing (reverence) □ **twirling:** making (it) turn quickly □ **cap:** type of hat □ **forefinger:** index finger

matter: question □ **pardon:** forgive, forgave, forgiven

wrinkling: with wrinkles, lines on his **forehead** (part of face above eyes) □ **buttoning:** to button; a button

edge: the limit of (sth.); the edge of a sofa, a table...

placed: put, set □ **knee(s):** where the leg bends

sharply: severely, in a sharp tone (of voice)

deny: say it is not true; you needn't deny it or you don't need to deny it; a need; needless to say

waved...: moved his arms up and down (to disapprove)

was a short, stout man, with a round face. His underlip stuck out aggressively.

'It's awful,' he said. 'Are you never going to pull yourself together? I suppose it's money you want.'

'That's not a charitable way of putting it, father. For a man in my condition who has been the unfortunate victim of... of cruel circumstances, I take it as an insult to be...'

He straightened himself and began to splutter.

'That's all rot,' said the priest. 'Listen. It's only last
10 night I was talking to Mr. Higgins and he told me about your disgraceful and thankless conduct. What did you do with the parcel of groceries he sent to your lodgings?'

'I dropped the contents at his hall door in his presence,' said Reddon, looking at the floor and sitting very motionless.

'Why, may I ask?'

'Because I am a gentleman and I refuse to accept charity from a shopkeeper whom I don't consider my social equal, an outsider, a mere nobody.'

20 The priest crossed his arms and stared at Reddon angrily.

'I've a good mind to kick you out the door and set my dogs after you,' he said bitterly.

Reddon suddenly burst into tears. He pulled out a handkerchief and pressed it to his eyes with both hands. His cap fell to the floor. He shook with emotion. The priest glared at him.

'Yes. I've a good mind to do it,' he continued. 'You're an unmitigated scoundrel and I know your kind. You feel
30 insulted at this good man's charity, and now I'm going to tell you why he sent you that grocery. He sent it because he saw you stealing a rasher of bacon out of his shop that

short: small □ **stout:** corpulent □ **underlip:** lower lip
stuck out: was prominent
awful: horrible □ **pull yourself together:** control yourself, make an effort and stop drinking
way: manner □ **putting it:** saying it; how shall I put it?
condition: social position □ **unfortunate:** unlucky
to be... (treated like that, in an uncharitable way)
straightened...: stood erect □ **splutter:** reject drops of saliva while speaking □ **rot:** nonsense □ **only last night:** not later than last night

disgraceful: dishonourable □ **thankless:** full of ingratitude
parcel: package □ **groceries:** tea, sugar, butter...
dropped: let fall □ **contents:** what the parcel contained
floor: surface of a room on which one stands or walks
motionless: without any movement, quite still
may I ask?: if I may ask (says the priest ironically)
gentleman: a man of honourable behaviour ("conduct")
shopkeeper: here a grocer (who sells "groceries")
outsider: stranger □ **a mere nobody:** just nobody, of no importance at all □ **stared at...:** looked fixedly at
angrily: angry with (sb.); angry at (sth.) (very displeased)
I have a good mind (a strong wish) **to** □ **kick:** hit with foot
bitterly: with animosity, reproachfully
burst into tears: suddenly started crying (or weeping)
handkerchief: piece of cotton (to dry his eyes with)
shook with emotion: trembled (with!); shake, shook, shaken
glared at him: looked angrily at...; a glare, an angry look

unmitigated: absolute □ **scoundrel:** unscrupulous man □ **kind:** people of your kind (sort) □ **insulted at:** notice "at"
grocery: groceries; grocery (usually) = grocer's shop
stealing: robbing □ **rasher:** very thin slice; slice of bread

159

morning and he took pity on you.   You are not too proud
to steal from a man but you won't take charity from
him.   You won't take charity from Mr. Higgins, but you'll
come to me for money and God knows I've little enough
to spare for myself, not to mention any old coppers I've got
for the deserving poor that are starving all around
me.   Oh! You low, heartless wretch.   I... I...   I don't
even pity you.   You are beyond pity.'

The priest stopped breathlessly.   He went over to the
10 window and looked out, clutching his hands nervously
behind his back. Reddon raised his head and his mournful,
bloodshot eyes stared at the priest's back.   His lips
trembled for some moments and then he spoke.

'Father Waters,' he said pompously, with hanging lower
lip, 'would you kindly allow me to defend myself?'

The priest did not reply or move.   The ex-schoolmaster
drew himself up, straightened his shoulders and put one
hand on his knee.

'You deal with facts, Father Waters, but I deal with
20 something that is more powerful than facts and that is the
curse that is upon me.'

'Rot,' said the priest, without moving.

'So be it,' said the schoolmaster. 'Amen I say to that.   It's
all rot.   I'm all rot and everything is all rot.   If I held my
position and if the inspector had not sent a report of
drunkenness to headquarters, I'd be still a schoolmaster,
but what would that amount to?   Nothing but rot.   There
would be still drunkards and unfortunate wretches and
liars and scoundrels.   If it's not me it's someone else.   I'm
30 not responsible.   I may be a liar and a thief and an
ungrateful scoundrel, but I'm still a gentleman, and a
gentleman never accepts charity.   I came to you because I

took pity on you: pitied you □ **proud:** self-satisfied
steal: steal (sth. *from* sb.); rob (sb. *of* sth.); steal, stole, stolen
you won't...: you'll... (such is your nature) (≠ future)

to spare: that I can do without □ **copper(s):** piece (money)
deserving: deserve, merit □ **starving:** having too little to eat
low: ignoble □ **heartless:** cruel □ **wretch:** good-for-nothing
beyond: outside the limits of (nobody can pity you)
breathlessly: breathing (taking in air) with difficulty
clutching: holding firmly, tightly
raised his head to look up; raise, lift, move upwards

hanging: hang, hung, hung □ **lower lip:** ≠ upper lip (p. 158 l. 1)
kindly: kindheartedly □ **allow me to:** give me permission to
reply: answer; to reply, to answer □ **move:** make a movement
drew himself up: stood erect, upright, proudly

you deal with (are concerned with) **facts:** you treat facts
powerful: full of power, force, very strong (≠ powerless)
curse: malediction, adversity, calamity, misfortune
rot: (originally) *pourriture*; rotten, *pourri*
so be it: all right, let's admit it (that it is all rot)
rot: (here) (sb. or sth.) of no value at all (p. 158 l. 9)
position (in society) □ **sent:** send, sent, sent
headquarters: office from which activities are controlled
what...amount to: what would the result be? □ **but:** except

liar(s): one who tells lies; tell lies ≠ speak the truth
responsible (*for* sth.) □ **thief:** robber, one who steals things
ungrateful: thankless (≠ grateful, thankful)

161

considered that you are something beyond me, something apart from the rest of the people, not a man but something,' he waved his hand and glanced around wildly, 'something apart. I may be wrong, but what are you for if not to stand between me and myself? Your business is to deal with drunkards and scoundrels and thieves. Yes. If there are no drunkards and scoundrels and thieves, then what is your business? If there are no poor and no sick, what use are you? You belong to me because I am a drunkard. That's 10 my way of looking at it. That's why I come to you for money and kick Higgins's groceries in through his hall door.'

He stood up arrogantly, swaying slightly, drunk through the efforts of his outburst. He pulled himself up very fiercely and stood waiting for the priest to turn round. But the priest did not move. His hands were still clutching. His short, broad back was trembling slightly.

'I have the honour to bid you good-day, Father Waters,' said Reddon.

20 He stepped back and made a pompous bow, which almost brought him to his knees. Then he walked stiffly towards the door.

'Come here,' said the priest gruffly. He put his hand in his pocket and held out two half-crown pieces. As soon as Reddon saw the money his eyes glittered. He shuffled over, trembling and licking his lips, his quivering right hand held out for the money. He grabbed it and put the coins to his lips. Then he backed to the door quickly, bowing and simpering, his face in a paroxysm of delight. His 30 whole being had changed and he was now a cunning, fawning drunkard, sneaking away with the price of another debauch. He passed out of the door noiselessly, without

beyond me: (here) more than me; beyond Bath, farther than...

glanced: took a quick look ☐ **wildly:** as if he were mad
be wrong: ≠ be right ☐ **stand...:** help me solve my problems
business: job, work, mission
thieves: plural of words ending in f! (handkerchie*f*s!)

what use *are* you?: use, useful; useless
you belong to me: you are at my disposal; belong to, be the property
of ☐ **looking at:** (mentally) considering, judging (things)
kick in: into the house ☐ **Higgins's house** or **Higgins' house**

swaying: swinging from side to side ☐ **slightly:** a little
outburst: long angry speech ☐ **pulled...,** to control balance
fiercely: violently
still indicates continuation; **again** indicates repetition
broad: wide, large across; broad-shouldered
to bid you good day: a "pompous" alternative for "to say goodbye
to you"; bid (sb.) farewell, bid (sb.) good morning...
stepped: walked; a step, a movement of the foot in walking
almost: very nearly ☐ **stiffly:** in a stiff (rigid) manner
towards: in the direction of
gruffly: in a gruff (abrupt, rough, stern) manner
half-crown: two shillings and six pence ☐ **piece(s):** coin
glittered: shone brightly ☐ **shuffled:** walked without raising feet
properly ☐ **licking:** lick, *lécher* ☐ **quivering:** trembling
grabbed: seized (it) with a sudden rough movement
backed: walked backwards (*à reculons*) ☐ **bowing:** making a bow
simpering: smile in silly unnatural way ☐ **delight:** great joy
whole: entire, complete ☐ **cunning** (as a fox): (too) clever
fawning (upon sb.): flattering to get (sth.) ☐ **sneaking:** walking
furtively ☐ **...debauch:** (here) money ("price") to drink again

utterring a word of thanks, but his lips kept moving, forming some inarticulate words.

The priest never turned his face from the window. He stood still, clutching his hands behind his back. But tears were rolling down his cheeks and he was thinking: 'What am I to do? He'll come again in a few days and the same thing will happen.'

uttering a word: saying a word □ **kept moving:** went on moving
inarticulate: not clear or distinct

still: without movement or sound □ **tear(s):** shed tears, cry
cheek(s): part of the face between the nose and the ears
what am I to do? = I don't know what to do (he's lost)
happen: take place, occur

Grammaire au fil des nouvelles

Traduisez les phrases suivantes inspirées du texte (le premier chiffre renvoie aux pages, les suivants aux lignes) :

Il comptait sur *une heure de repos* avant le dîner (génitif pour exprimer la durée ; emploi de **the**, 156.4,5).

Reddon, ancien instituteur, ivrogne notoire, entra lourdement dans la pièce (noms en apposition, 156.9).

Il ferma tranquillement la porte (place de l'adverbe, 156.19).

Pour un homme de ma condition, qui a été la malheureuse victime de circonstances cruelles... (relatif, 158.6).

Reddon était assis, immobile (positions du corps, 158.14).

Le prêtre croisa *les* bras. Reddon leva *la* tête (noms de parties du corps précédés de..., 158.20 et 160.11).

De ses deux mains il pressa son mouchoir contre ses yeux (**both**, 158.25).

Je vais te dire pourquoi il t'a porté ces articles d'épicerie (futur immédiat, 158.30).

...sans parler de vieilles pièces que je garde pour les pauvres méritants (infinitif négatif ; adjectifs substantivés, 160.5,6).

Permettez-moi de me défendre (pronoms réfléchis, 160.15).

Il y aurait toujours des ivrognes (expression de la continuation, 160.27,28).

Je suis peut-être un menteur et un voleur... J'ai peut-être tort (expression de la probabilité, 160.30 et 162.4).

Il se tenait debout, attendant que le prêtre se retourne (proposition infinitive introduite par **for** avec **wait**, 162.15).

Il passa par la porte sans prononcer un mot de remerciement mais ses lèvres continuaient de remuer (emplois du gérondif, 162.32 et 164.1).

Que vais-je faire ? Il reviendra dans *quelques* jours et la même chose se produira (futur de projet, 164.6).

THE FLY

by Katherine Mansfield (1888-1923)

Katherine Mansfield was born in New Zealand but she completed her education in England. She planned a musical career but married in 1909 and did not fulfil her ambition. She was divorced from her husband in 1913 and in 1918 married John Middleton Murry, the famous literary critic. Her first book, *In a German Pension,* was published in 1911. She contracted tuberculosis in 1917, which made it necessary for her to travel much in the South of France and in Germany. Her reputation as a brilliant short story writer was established with her second volume, *Bliss* (1920). Her third collection, *The Garden Party*, appeared in 1922. After her early death in Fontainebleau two more collections of her stories were published as well as her *Letters* and her *Journal,* most of them now available in Penguin Books.

Katherine Mansfield is traditionally compared to Chekhov in her treatment of apparently unimportant incidents in every day life. Her stories are sensitive revelations of human behaviour in quite ordinary situations. They are often cruelly pessimistic.

"Y'are very snug in here", piped old Mr. Woodifield, and he peered out of the great, green-leathern arm-chair by his friend the boss's desk as a baby peers out of its pram. His talk was over; it was time for him to be off. But he did not want to go. Since he had retired, since his... stroke, the wife and the girls kept him boxed up in the house every day of the week except Tuesday. On Tuesday he was dressed and brushed and allowed to cut back to the City for the day. Though what he did there the wife and girls
10 couldn't imagine. Made a nuisance of himself to his friends, they supposed... Well, perhaps so. All the same, we cling to our last pleasures as the tree clings to its last leaves. So there sat old Woodifield, smoking a cigar and staring almost greedily at the boss, who rolled in his office chair, stout, rosy, five years older than he, and still going strong, still at the helm. It did one good to see him.

Wistfully, admiringly, the old voice added, "It's snug in here, upon my word!"

20 "Yes, it's comfortable enough", agreed the boss, and he flipped the *Financial Times* with a paper-knife. As a matter of fact he was proud of his room; he liked to have it admired, especially by old Woodifield. It gave him a feeling of deep, solid satisfaction to be planted there in the midst of it in full view of that frail old figure in the muffler.

"I've had it done up lately", he explained, as he had explained for the past —how many?— weeks. "New carpet", and he pointed to the bright red carpet with a
30 pattern of large white rings. "New furniture", and he nodded towards the massive bookcase and the table with legs like twisted treacle. "Electric heating!" He waved

snug: comfortable, cosy □ **piped:** spoke in a high childish voice
peered: scrutinized □ **leathern:** made of leather *(cuir)* □ **by:** near
boss: (fam.) employer □ **desk:** writing desk or table □ **pram:** baby
carriage □ **talk:** conversation □ **over:** finished □ **to be off:** to go
retired: stopped working, because of age □ **stroke:** (heart) attack
boxed up: boxed in, kept like in a box, shut up, locked up
Tuesday: with a capital T!
brushed: made clean with a brush *(brosse)* □ **allowed to cut
back:** given permission to return □ **City:** London business centre
made a nuisance...: irritated, annoyed his friends
perhaps so: perhaps it was the case (he did annoy them)
all the same: yet, however □ **cling to:** hold firmly on to
last: ≠ first □ **so...:** so old Woodifield was sitting there
staring: looking fixedly □ **greedily:** avidly, with envy
stout: corpulent, fat ≠ thin □ **rosy:** indicating good health
...helm: still at the head of his firm □ **it did one good...:**
it was a real pleasure...; do (sb.) good ≠ do (sb.) harm, hurt
wistfully: with a mixture of regret and envy □ **added:** addition ≠ subtraction □ **upon my word:** on my honour
agreed: had the same opinion; agree with ≠ disagree with
flipped: gave a sudden tap to □ **as a matter of fact:** in fact
proud: showing too much satisfaction or pride, arrogant

feeling: impression □ **deep:** profound □ **solid:** complete, full
midst: centre □ **in full view:** fully seen by that weak (frail) old man
in the **muffler** scarf *(écharpe)*
done up lately: painted and repaired recently
explained: made clear; explanation
pointed to: showed with his fingers □ **bright:** full of light
pattern: ornamental design □ **ring(s):** circle □ **furniture:** chairs,
tables, beds... □ **nodded:** indicated with his head
twisted: contorted □ **treacle:** *mélasse* □ **waved:** moved his hand

169

almost exultantly towards the five transparent, pearly sausages glowing so softly in the tilted copper pan.

But he did not draw old Woodifield's attention to the photograph over the table of a grave-looking boy in uniform standing in one of those spectral photographers' parks with photographers' storm-clouds behind him. It was not new. It had been there for over six years.

"There was something I wanted to tell you", said old Woodifield, and his eyes grew dim remembering. "Now
10 what was it? I had it in my mind when I started out this morning." His hands began to tremble, and patches of red showed above his beard.

Poor old chap, he's on his last pins, thought the boss. And, feeling kindly, he winked at the old man, and said jokingly, "I tell you what. I've got a little drop of something here that'll do you good before you go out into the cold again. It's beautiful stuff. It wouldn't hurt a child." He took a key off his watch-chain, unlocked a cupboard below his desk, and drew forth a dark, squat
20 bottle. "That's the medicine", said he. "And the man from whom I got it told me on the strict Q.T. it came from the cellars at Windsor Castle."

Old Woodifield's mouth fell open at the sight. He couldn't have looked more surprised if the boss had produced a rabbit.

"It's whisky, ain't it?" he piped feebly.

The boss turned the bottle and lovingly showed him the label. Whisky it was.

"D'you know", said he, peering up at the boss
30 wonderingly, "they won't let me touch it at home." And he looked as though he was going to cry.

"Ah, that's where we know a bit more than the ladies",

towards: in the direction of ☐ **pearly:** like pearls *(perles)*
glowing: red, shining ☐ **tilted:** inclined, leaning ☐ **copper pan:**
cooking pot made of copper, a reddish metal, (here) the radiator
whose elements are compared to "sausages" glowing "softly",
with very little or no noise
storm-clouds: dark clouds in the sky announcing violent weather
with wind, rain and lightning ☐ **over:** more than (≠ under)

grew dim: became dark; dim ≠ bright ☐ **now:** now then! let's see!
I had it in my mind: I could still remember it, it hadn't got out of
my head ☐ **patches:** marks, spots
showed: could be seen ☐ **beard:** hair on lower part of face
chap: (fam.) man, fellow ☐ **on his last pins:** going to die soon
kindly: showing sympathy ☐ **winked:** shut and opened one eye
quickly ☐ **jokingly:** to make him laugh ☐ **I tell you what:** I'll tell
you one thing ☐ **...something:** something nice to drink
beautiful stuff: (fam.) a good thing ☐ **hurt:** cause pain, injure
key: a key to a door ☐ **unlocked:** opened with a key
below: under ≠ above ☐ **drew forth:** took out ☐ **squat:** short
medicine: substance given by doctors to patients to cure them
on the strict Q.T.: quite confidentially (Q.T. = quiet)
cellar(s): underground room where wine is kept ☐ **Windsor Castle:**
the Queen's residence near London ☐ **...fell open at the sight:**
opened wide as he saw the bottle; have a good eyesight
produced a rabbit: shown a rabbit from a hat like a magician
ain't it?: isn't it? ☐ **feebly:** weakly, in a very low voice
lovingly: in a loving way, appreciative of the whisky
label: piece of paper on bottle.. ☐ **whisky it was:** it really was
whisky, it was whisky indeed
wonderingly: wondering, asking himself why, with astonishment
as though: as if ☐ **cry:** let eyes fill with tears, weep
a bit: a little

cried the boss, swooping across for two tumblers that stood on the table with the water-bottle, and pouring a generous finger into each. "Drink it down. It'll do you good. And don't put any water with it. It's sacrilege to tamper with stuff like this. Ah!" He tossed off his, pulled out his handkerchief, hastily wiped his moustaches, and cocked an eye at old Woodifield, who was rolling his in his chaps.

The old man swallowed, was silent a moment, and then said faintly, "It's nutty!"

10 But it warmed him; it crept into his chill old brain—he remembered.

"That was it", he said, heaving himself out of his chair. "I thought you'd like to know. The girls were in Belgium last week having a look at poor Reggie's grave, and they happened to come across your boy's. They're quite near each other, it seems."

Old Woodifield paused, but the boss made no reply. Only a quiver in his eyelids showed that he heard.

"The girls were delighted with the way the place is kept",
20 piped the old voice. "Beautifully looked after. Couldn't be better if they were at home. You've not been across, have yer?"

"No, no!" For various reasons the boss had not been across.

"There's miles of it", quavered old Woodifield, "and it's all as neat as a garden. Flowers growing on all the graves. Nice broad paths." It was plain from his voice how much he liked a nice broad path.

The pause came again. Then the old man brightened
30 wonderfully.

"D'you know what the hotel made the girls pay for a pot of jam?" he piped. "Ten francs! Robbery, I call it. It

172

swooping... for: coming with a rush to take □ **tumbler(s):** glass

pouring: pouring whisky from the bottle into the glasses

finger: measure of alcoholic drink □ **do (sb.) good:** ≠ do (sb.) harm, hurt, injure □ **tamper with:** damage whisky with water

tossed off his: drank his (whisky) quickly, straight down

handkerchief: *mouchoir* □ **hastily:** quickly □ **cocked an eye:** looked sideways □ **rolling his** (whisky) □ **chaps:** *bajoues*

swallowed: drank down his whisky □ **silent:** keep silent!

faintly: feebly, weakly □ **nutty:** excellent, tasting like nuts

warmed: made him warm □ **crept into his chill old brain:** slowly came to (impregnated) his cold (chill) old brain *(cerveau)*

heaving...: standing up with effort or difficulty

grave: place in a cemetery where (sb.) is buried, tomb

they happened to come across...: they saw your boy's (grave) accidentally, by chance; I happened to see him in the street

old Woodifield: no article! □ **paused:** stopped speaking

reply: answer □ **quiver:** trembling movement □ **eyelid(s):** *paupière*

delighted with: very pleased with □ **way:** manner □ **kept:** kept in good order, looked after, taken care of

at home: (here) in England □ **across:** across, over to Belgium

have yer?: have you? ("yer", bad pronunciation of "you")

for various reasons: for different reasons; the reason *why*...

miles of it: lots of graves □ **quavered:** trembled, shook (voice)

neat: in perfect order, clean and tidy

broad: wide ≠ narrow □ **path(s):** way, passage □ **plain:** evident, clear, obvious; in plain words, frankly

pause: short break (in conversation...) □ **brightened:** looked happy, cheerful; his face brightened as he heard the good news

pay for: the girls paid ten francs for the pot (for!)

jam: *confiture* □ **robbery:** rob (sb *of* sth.), steal (sth. *from* sb.)

173

was a little pot, so Gertrude says, no bigger than a half-crown. And she hadn't taken more than a spoonful when they charged her ten francs. Gertrude brought the pot away with her to teach 'em a lesson. Quite right, too; it's trading on our feelings. They think because we're over there having a look round we're ready to pay anything. That's what it is." And he turned towards the door.

"Quite right, quite right!" cried the boss, though what was quite right he hadn't the least idea. He came round by his desk, followed the shuffling footsteps to the door, and saw the old fellow out. Woodifield was gone.

For a long moment the boss stayed, staring at nothing, while the grey-haired office messenger, watching him, dodged in and out of his cubby-hole like a dog that expects to be taken for a run. Then: "I'll see nobody for half an hour, Macey", said the boss. "Understand? Nobody at all."

"Very good, sir."

20   The door shut, the firm heavy steps recrossed the bright carpet, the fat body plumped down in the spring chair, and leaning forward, the boss covered his face with his hands. He wanted, he intended, he had arranged to weep...

It had been a terrible shock to him when old Woodifield sprang that remark upon him about the boy's grave. It was exactly as though the earth had opened and he had seen the boy lying there with Woodifield's girls staring down at him. For it was strange. Although over six years had passed away, the boss never thought of the boy except as lying unchanged, unblemished in his uniform, asleep for ever. "My son!" groaned the boss. But no tears came

so...: that's what Gertrude says, according to Gertrude
halfcrown: piece, coin (= 2 shillings and six pence) □ **spoonful:**
as much as a spoon can hold □ **charged:** asked in payment;
the charge, the price □ **right:** just, morally good ≠ wrong
trading on: taking a wrong advantage of..., to make money
having a look round: visiting the place □ **ready to:** prepared to
that's what it is: that's what they think □ **he turned towards:** he
turned (no reflexive pronoun!) in the direction of
quite right!: absolutely! definitely! □ **though:** although
he hadn't the least idea: he had no idea at all
by: near □ **followed:** came after □ **shuffling:** moving slowly,
with effort □ **saw... out:** accompanied the old man out
stayed: stood, remained there □ **staring:** looking fixedly
office: room (≠ desk) □ **messenger:** one who carries messages
dodged...: went quickly in and out □ **cubby hole:** snug place
a run: take a dog for a run □ **half an hour:** a quarter of an hour,
an hour and a half (position of a, an) □ **understand?:** do you
understand? (the boss is rather brusque)

heavy: slow, difficult □ **step(s):** movement of foot in walking
fat: corpulent □ **plumped down:** fell suddenly □ **spring:** *ressort*
leaning: you lean out of a window □ **forward(s):** ≠ backwards
he intended to: he had the intention of + ing
weep: let eyes fill with tears, cry; weep, wept, wept
to: a shock *to* him, bad news *to* him, a surprise *to* him
sprang... on: told him that suddenly, unexpectedly, point-blank
as though: as if □ **the earth:** the planet we live on
lying: lie, lay, lain (≠ lay, laid, laid; lay (sth.) on the table)
for: because □ **strange:** odd □ **over:** more than (≠ under)
thought of: think, thought, thought (of!)
unblemished: intact, undamaged, unspoiled □ **asleep:** sleeping
for ever: eternally □ **groaned:** made a deep sound in despair

yet.   In the past, in the first months and even years after
the boy's death, he had only to say those words to be
overcome by such grief that nothing short of a violent fit of
weeping could relieve him.   Time, he had declared then, he
had told everybody, could make no difference.   Other men
perhaps might recover, might live their loss down, but not
he.   How was it possible?   His boy was an only
son.   Ever since his birth the boss had worked at building
up this business for him; it had no other meaning if it was
10 not for the boy.   Life itself had come to have no other
meaning.   How on earth could he have slaved, denied
himself, kept going all those years without the promise for
ever before him of the boy's stepping into his shoes and
carrying on where he left off?

And that promise had been so near being fulfilled.   The
boy had been in the office learning the ropes for a year
before the war.   Every morning they had started off
together; they had come back by the same train.   And
what congratulations he had received as the boy's
20 father!   No wonder; he had taken to it marvellously.   As
to his popularity with the staff, every man jack of them
down to old Macey couldn't make enough of the
boy.   And he wasn't in the least spoilt.   No, he was just
his bright natural self, with the right word for everybody,
with that boyish look and his habit of saying, "Simply
splendid!"

But all that was over and done with as though it never
had been.   The day had come when Macey had handed
him the telegram that brought the whole place crashing
30 about his head.   "Deeply regret to inform you..."   And
he had left the office a broken man, with his life in ruins.

Six years ago, six years... How quickly time passed!   It

months: January is a month □ **even:** even a child knows that
death: end of life; die in an accident; be dead
overcome: defeated □ **grief:** affliction □ **nothing short...:** nothing
less than a violent access (a fit) □ **relieve:** bring relief, consolation
to □ **make no difference:** change nothing
recover: come back to normal state □ **live their loss down:** live long
enough to forget the death of their sons (to lose) □ **only:** without
brothers or sisters □ **since his birth:** since he was born
business: commercial enterprise □ **meaning:** sense, significance

how on earth... slaved... denied himself: how could he possibly have
worked hard (like a slave), made sacrifices □ **kept going:** continued
working □ **stepping into his shoes:** replacing him
carrying on: continuing □ **left off:** gave up working, retired
that promise...: the expectation had nearly come true, the son nearly
replaced his father □ **the ropes:** (fam.) the (business)
techniques, the procedures □ **started off:** started off to work

congratulations: compliments; congratulate (sb. *on* sth.)
no wonder: it was not surprising □ **taken to it:** taken an interest in
the job □ **as to:** *quant à* □ **staff:** personnel □ **every man jack:**
everyone without exception □ **...make enough of:** couldn't like him
more □ **n't in the least spoilt:** not spoilt at all (as only children often
are) □ **his bright...:** himself, jovial, with a nice word for everybody
boyish look... habit: the air, the appearance of a young boy; habit,
habitual, customary
over and done with: finished for good, for ever
handed him: passed him (with his hand)
brought the whole place crashing: caused the whole place to come
to ruin, psychologically speaking; car crash □ **deeply:** deep,
profound □ **a broken man:** a man reduced to despair
how quickly time passed!: the phrase is "Time flies!"

might have happened yesterday. The boss took his hands from his face; he was puzzled. Something seemed to be wrong with him. He wasn't feeling as he wanted to feel. He decided to get up and have a look at the boy's photograph. But it wasn't a favourite photograph of his; the expression was unnatural. It was cold, even stern-looking. The boy had never looked like that.

At that moment the boss noticed that a fly had fallen into his broad inkpot, and was trying feebly but desperately to 10 clamber out again. Help! help! said those struggling legs. But the sides of the inkpot were wet and slippery; it fell back again and began to swim. The boss took up a pen, picked the fly out of the ink, and shook it on to a piece of blotting-paper. For a fraction of a second it lay still on the dark patch that oozed round it. Then the front legs waved, took hold, and, pulling its small, sodden body up, it began the immense task of cleaning the ink from its wings. Over and under, over and under, went a leg along a wing as the stone goes over and under the scythe. Then 20 there was a pause, while the fly, seeming to stand on the tips of its toes, tried to expand first one wing and then the other. It succeeded at last, and, sitting down, it began, like a minute cat, to clean its face. Now one could imagine that the little front legs rubbed against each other lightly, joyfully. The horrible danger was over; it had escaped; it was ready for life again.

But just then the boss had an idea. He plunged his pen back into the ink, leaned his thick wrist on the blotting-paper, and as the fly tried its wings down came a great heavy 30 blot. What would it make of that? What indeed! The little beggar seemed absolutely cowed, stunned, and afraid to move because of what would happen next. But then, as

178

happened: taken place, occurred (speaking about an event)
puzzled: perplexed, baffled; a puzzling problem
wrong: out of order, in a bad condition (≠ right): what's wrong with you? there's nothing wrong with me, I'm all right
a favourite photograph of his: one of his favourite photographs
stern-looking: looking severe, strict, hard, unkind
looked like: look like (sb.), resemble (sb.) (no preposition!)
noticed: paid attention to, took notice of □ **fly:** *mouche*
broad: big □ **inkpot:** container for ink *(encre)*, ink bottle
clamber out: get out with effort □ **struggling:** fighting
wet: saturated with ink, damp (≠ dry) □ **slippery:** difficult to stand on without slipping (you slip on a banana skin)
pen: instrument for writing with ink □ **shook:** moved quickly, violently □ **blotting-paper:** *papier buvard* □ **still:** without movement □ **patch:** mark □ **oozed:** grew slowly larger
waved...: moved up and down, held on to the paper □ **sodden:** wet through, very wet □ **task:** work, job □ **cleaning:** making clean (≠ dirty) □ **wing(s):** a fly has two wings to fly with
stone: whetstone *(pierre à aiguiser)* □ **scythe:** *faux*
while: during the moment that □ **tip(s):** end, fingertip
toe(s): each digit of foot □ **expand:** extend, stretch
succeeded: succeed in + ing; success □ **at (long) last:** in the end □ **minute:** very small, tiny □ **one:** you, any person
rubbed: rub; rubbing, friction □ **lightly:** slowly, gently
escaped: escape from danger, escape from prison (from!)

had an idea: an idea occurred to him □ **plunged:** dipped
leaned: put, rested □ **thick:** big □ **wrist:** joint between hand and arm
tried: tested □ **down...:** a very big drop of ink fell
make of: react to □ **what indeed!** yes, what!
beggar: (fam.) fellow, man □ **cowed:** terrified □ **stunned:** knocked out, made unconscious, dazed □ **next:** after that, afterwards

if painfully, it dragged itself forward. The front legs waved, caught hold, and, more slowly this time, the task began from the beginning.

He's a plucky little devil, thought the boss, and he felt a real admiration for the fly's courage. That was the way to tackle things; that was the right spirit. Never say die; it was only a question of... But the fly had again finished its laborious task, and the boss had just time to refill his pen, to shake fair and square on the new-cleaned body yet
10 another dark drop. What about it this time? A painful moment of suspense followed. But behold, the front legs were again waving; the boss felt a rush of relief. He leaned over the fly and said to it tenderly, "You artful little b..." And he actually had the brilliant notion of breathing on it to help the drying process. All the same, there was something timid and weak about its efforts now, and the boss decided that this time should be the last, as he dipped the pen deep into the inkpot.

It was. The last blot fell on the soaked blotting-paper,
20 and the draggled fly lay in it and did not stir. The back legs were stuck to the body; the front legs were not to be seen.

"Come on", said the boss. "Look sharp!" And he stirred it with his pen—in vain. Nothing happened or was likely to happen. The fly was dead.

The boss lifted the corpse on the end of the paper-knife and flung it into the waste-paper basket. But such a grinding feeling of wretchedness seized him that he felt positively frightened. He started forward and pressed the
30 bell for Macey.

"Bring me some fresh blotting-paper", he said sternly, "and look sharp about it." And while the old dog padded

painfully: with effort, suffering □ **dragged itself...:** moved on with difficulty □ **caught hold:** "took hold" □ **this time:** on this occasion; come another time □ **beginning:** ≠ end

plucky: brave and determined □ **devil:** (fam.) fellow, man

that was the way: that was the right method, manner

tackle: attack (problem) □ **spirit:** attitude □ **never say die:** never lose courage, never give up

laborious: difficult, tiring □ **refill:** fill again; full ≠ empty

fair and square: directly, straight, right, bang (on...)

what about it?: what would happen this time?

behold: (old and literary) look, see, take notice

rush: sudden movement □ **relief:** stopping of tension or pain

artful: too clever or intelligent ≠ artless, simple, innocent

b...: "beggar" □ **actually:** in fact □ **notion:** idea □ **breathing...:** blowing on it to help it get dry □ **all the same:** in spite of this, yet, however □ **weak:** ≠ strong, powerful

dipped: put sth into a liquid, "plunge" (p. 178 l. 27)

last: ≠ first; last but not least □ **soaked:** wet through

draggled: wet and dirty □ **stir:** move ≠ keep still

stuck: fixed; stick a stamp on an envelope □ **were not to be seen:** could not be seen

come on: come on! make an effort! □ **look sharp!:** hurry up!

stirred: caused to move; a breeze stirred the leaves

likely to happen: expected to happen; it is likely to rain

lifted: took up, raised □ **corpse:** dead body

flung: threw suddenly □ **waste-paper:** paper thrown away

grinding: oppressive □ **wretchedness:** great unhappiness

positively: really □ **frightened:** terrified □ **pressed the bell for Macey:** ...to make Macey come; door bell, church bell (ringing)

fresh: clean and new □ **sternly:** severely, harshly

padded away: went away noiselessly, walked away softly

away he fell to wondering what it was he had been thinking about before.   What was it?   It was... He took out his handkerchief and passed it inside his collar.   For the life of him he could not remember.

he fell to wondering: he began to ask himself; fall to doing (sth.), begin to do (sth.)

inside: ≠ outside □ **collar:** shirt collar □ **for the life of him...:** (intensive) he could not remember at all

Grammaire au fil des nouvelles

Traduisez les phrases suivantes inspirées du texte (le premier chiffre renvoie aux pages, les suivants aux lignes) :

"C'est très confortable ici", dit *le vieux Woodifield* d'une voix aiguë (problème de l'article avec noms de personne précédés d'un adjectif familier, 168.1).

Il était temps qu'il s'en aille (proposition infinitive introduite par **for** après certains noms ou adjectifs, 168.4).

Le mardi *on* l'habillait et *on* le brossait et *on* l'autorisait à retourner à la City (voix passive, 168.7).

Sa femme ne pouvait s'imaginer *ce qu'*il y faisait (168.9).

Cela *vous* faisait du bien de le voir (sens général, universel de **one**, 168.16).

"C'est *assez* confortable", acquiesça le patron (168.20).

J'ai fait retaper mon bureau (**have**+... 168.27).

La photo *était* là *depuis* plus de six ans (170.7).

On eût dit qu'il allait pleurer (futur immédiat, 170.31).

La semaine dernière, les filles ont vu la tombe de Reggie et *celle de* votre gars (172.13,14,15).

C'est très bien tenu (verbes à particule au passif, 172.20).

Elle a emporté le pot de confiture *pour* leur faire la leçon (174.3).

Ils croient que nous sommes disposés à payer *n'importe quoi...* Je ne veux voir personne pendant une demi-heure (**some, any, no** et composés; place de **a, an**, 174.6 et 174.16).

Penché en avant, le patron se couvrit le visage de ses mains (positions du corps; parties du corps et possessifs, 174.22).

Comment *aurait-il pu* se priver?... (réfléchis, 176.11)... Cela *aurait pu* arriver hier (178.1).

Tous les matins ils étaient partis ensemble (176.17).

Comme le temps passait vite! (**how** exclamatif, 176.32).

Les petites pattes de devant se frottaient l'une contre l'autre (pronoms réciproques, 178.24).

Il y avait *quelque chose de timide* dans ses efforts (180.15).

THE LAST LEAF

by O. Henry (1862-1910)

William Sidney Porter, who signed his work with the nom de plume O. Henry, was born in North Carolina, the son of a doctor.   As a young man he moved to Texas for his health.   He spent a couple of years on a ranch, then worked in an office and later in a bank where he was charged with stealing money.   He tried to escape into Central America but was eventually sent to prison for a short time.   While there, he began to contribute short stories to magazines.   They have been collected in such volumes as *The Four Million*, *Cabbages and Kings*, and *The Voice of the City*. Selections are available in Minster Classics London and Washington Square Press published by Pocket Books, New York.

O. Henry's reputation stands upon his short stories alone (some six hundred).   The settings are either the wild West and the South or large cities notably New York, "Bagdad-on-the-Subway".   The characters are often immoral good-for-notings.   The story itself is very carefully constructed with a surprise ending (like in *The Last Leaf*).

In a little district west of Washington Square the streets have run crazy and broken themselves into small strips called "places". These "places" make strange angles and curves. One street crosses itself a time or two. An artist once discovered a valuable possibility in this street. Suppose a collector with a bill for paints, paper and canvas should, in traversing this route, suddenly meet himself coming back, without a cent having been paid on account!

10 So, to quaint old Greenwich Village the art people soon came prowling, hunting for north windows and eighteenth-century gables and Dutch attics and low rents. Then they imported some pewter mugs and a chafing dish or two from Sixth Avenue, and became a "colony".

At the top of a squatty, three-story brick Sue and Johnsy had their studio. "Johnsy" was familiar for Joanna. One was from Maine; the other from California. They had met at the *table d'hôte* of an Eighth Street "Delmonico's", and found their tastes in art, chicory salad 20 and bishop sleeves so congenial that the joint studio resulted.

That was in May. In November a cold, unseen stranger, whom the doctors called Pneumonia, stalked about the colony, touching one here and there with his icy fingers. Over on the east side this ravager strode boldly, smiting his victims by scores, but his feet trod slowly through the maze of the narrow and moss-grown "places".

Mr. Pneumonia was not what you would call a chivalric 30 old gentleman. A mite of a little woman with blood thinned by California zephyrs was hardly fair game for the red-fisted, short-breathed old duffer. But Johnsy he

186

district: part of a town, area □ **street(s):** road (also in a town)

run crazy: gone mad □ **strip (s):** long, narrow piece of land...

place(s): the usual word is "square" or "circus

curve: arc, circle; curved line □ **crosses itself:** intersects; cross, intersection □ **once:** one day (not "a"!)

collector: one who collects debts, taxes □ **bill:** money to be paid

canvas: a painter paints on a canvas □ **route:** itinerary

...himself: come face to face with himself □ **cent: 100 cents =** 1 dollar □ **account:** bank account, current account

quaint: old and picturesque □ **soon:** in a short time

prowling, hunting: going about secretely, looking for...

gable(s): *pignon* □ **attic(s)** *grenier* □ **rent(s):** *loyer*

pewter: *étain* □ **mug(s):** beer... mug (to drink in) □ **chafing dish:** used for cooking or keeping food warm

squat(ty): ≠ high □ **three-story brick (house):** a house with three stories or floors □ **studio:** workroom for a painter, a sculptor...

Maine: a state in the east of the U.S.A.

Delmonico's: (chain) restaurant □ **taste(s):** liking, interest

bishop sleeve(s): *manche à gigot* □ **congenial:** in harmony

resulted: as a result they decided to live together in the same studio

unseen: invisible □ **stranger:** (sb.) you do not know

stalked: walked in a self-important way

icy: very cold, like ice (water made solid by cold)

strode: walked with long steps □ **boldly:** resolutely

smiting: hitting, striking □ **score(s):** twenty □ **trod:** walked

maze: labyrinth □ **narrow:** ≠ wide, broad □ **moss-grown:** covered with moss ("A rolling stone gathers no moss")

call: name, describe(as) □ **chivalric:** honorable, courteous

a mite... woman: a very small woman □ **blood:** red liquid in body

thinned: made thin (≠ thick) □ **was... game:** unjustly inferior

fist: *poing* □ **breath:** *souffle* □ **duffer:** idiot, fool

smote; and she lay, scarcely moving, on her painted iron bedstead, looking through the small Dutch window-panes at the blank side of the next brick house.

One morning the busy doctor invited Sue into the hallway with a shaggy, gray eyebrow.

"She has one chance in—let us say, ten", he said, as he shook down the mercury in his clinical thermome-ter. "And that chance is for her to want to live. This way people have of lining-up on the side of the undertaker
10 makes the entire pharmacopoeia look silly. Your little lady has made up her mind that she's not going to get well. Has she anything on her mind?"

"She—she wanted to paint the Bay of Naples some day", said Sue.

"Paint?—bosh! Has she anything on her mind worth thinking about twice—a man, for instance?"

"A man?" said Sue, with a jew's-harp twang in her voice. "Is a man worth—but, no, doctor; there is nothing of the kind."
20 "Well, it is the weakness, then", said the doctor. "I will do all that science, so far as it may filter through my efforts, can accomplish. But whenever my patient begins to count the carriages in her funeral procession I subtract 50 per cent from the curative power of medicines. If you will get her to ask one question about the new winter styles in cloak sleeves I will promise you a one-in-five chance for her, instead of one in ten."

After the doctor had gone Sue went into the workroom and cried a Japanese napkin to a pulp. Then she
30 swaggered into Johnsy's room with her drawing board, whistling ragtime.

Johnsy, lay, scarcely making a ripple under the

188

scarcely moving: hardly making any movement □ **iron:** the most common metal □ **Dutch:** from Holland □ **window-panes:** are made of glass □ **blank:** empty, of no interest □ **next:** coming immediately after, following □ **hallway:** (Am.) hall

shaggy: thick, bushy □ **eyebrow:** arc of hair above the eye

she has one chance: she stands one chance (of surviving)

shook: shake, move up and down or from side to side

want: wish, desire □ **way:** method, manner

lining up: (Am.) queuing up □ **undertaker:** man in charge of funerals □ **pharmacopoeia:** medicines, drugs □ **silly:** ridiculous

has made up her mind: has decided □ **get well:** recover

... anything on her mind: anything that is preoccupying her

some day: one day (not a!), one day or other

bosh! nonsense! □ **worth...:** important enough...

twice: once, twice, three times... □ **for instance:** for example

jew's-harp: musical instrument (*guimbarde*) □ **twang:** nasal sound

worth: worth (thinking about); worth + ing: this film is worth seeing □ **nothing of the kind:** nothing of the sort

weakness: weak, unable to resist (≠ strong)

(in) so far as: *dans la mesure où* □ **filter:** make its way

whenever: every time that □ **count:** say the numbers in order

carriage(s): vehicle □ **subtract:** subtraction ≠ addition

power: ability to do (sth.) □ **get her...:** convince her...

cloak: coat; (theatre...) cloakroom for coats, hats...

sleeve(s): (of a coat...) cover the arms

instead of: in place of □ **one in ten:** one out of ten

cried... pulp: cried a lot □ **napkin:** serviette (when eating)

swaggered: walked in a self-satisfied way □ **drawing board:** drawing is an art; board, plank □ **whistling:** birds whistle

ripple: small movement (on surface of lake, sea...)

bedclothes, with her face toward the window. Sue stopped whistling, thinking she was asleep.

She arranged her board and began a pen-and-ink drawing to illustrate a magazine story. Young artists must pave their way to Art by drawing pictures for magazine stories that young authors write to pave their way to Literature.

As Sue was sketching a pair of elegant horseshow riding trousers and a monocle on the figure of the hero, an Idaho
10 cowboy, she heard a low sound, several times repeated. She went quickly to the bedside.

Johnsy's eyes were open wide. She was looking out the window and counting—counting backward.

"Twelve", she said, and a little later "eleven"; and then "ten", and "nine"; and then "eight" and "seven", almost together.

She looked solicitously out of the window. What was there to count? There was only a bare, dreary yard to be seen, and the blank side of the brick house twenty feet
20 away. An old, old, ivy vine, gnarled and decayed at the roots, climbed half way up the brick wall. The cold breath of autumn had stricken its leaves from the vine until its skeleton branches clung, almost bare, to the crumbling bricks.

"What is it, dear?" asked Sue.

"Six", said Johnsy, in almost a whisper. "They're falling faster now. Three days ago there were almost a hundred. It made my head ache to count them. But now it's easy. There goes another one. There are only five left
30 now."

"Five what, dear? Tell your Sudie."

"Leaves. On the ivy vine. When the last one falls I

190

bedclothes: (white) sheets, blankets... □ **toward(s):** in the direction of □ **asleep:** sleeping; fall asleep, go to sleep

pen: pointed piece of metal for writing □ **ink:** coloured liquid used for writing □ **drawing:** (here) picture in pencil...

by drawing: with the help of...; he succeeded by working hard; draw, drew, drawn □ **pave their way to art:** prepare their way...

sketching: drawing quickly □ **horseshow:** exhibition □ **riding trousers:** trousers worn by people on horseback □ **figure:** shape of the body, contour, human form □ **low:** ≠ loud (voice...)

bedside: bedside story read out to children at bedtime

open wide: fully, completely open □ **out the window:** (Am.) out of the window □ **counting backward(s):** "twelve, eleven, ten, nine... ≠ foreward(s)

almost together: practically without any interruption, uninterrupt-edly

solicitously: with anxiety; solicitous, anxious, concerned

bare: empty, not decorated □ **dreary:** sad, gloomy □ **yard:** children play in a school yard □ **feet:** 1 foot = 30,48 cm

ivy: *lierre* □ **vine:** plant □ **gnarled:** deformed □ **decayed:** dying

root(s): parts of tree in soil □ **climbed:** went up □ **breath:** (of air) wind □ **stricken...:** detached from

clung... to: held desperately to □ **bare:** leafless □ **crumbling:** breaking or falling into very small pieces

a whisper: a murmur; to whisper, to murmur (speak very softly)

faster: more rapidly

it made my head ache: it gave me a headache (continuous pain)

there are only five (leaves) left (on the vine), all the others have blown away; I've ten francs left; I have some money left; I've no money left, I've spent it all...

when the last one falls: present tense after when; last ≠ first

191

must go, too. I've known that for three days. Didn't the doctor tell you?"

"Oh, I never heard of such nonsense", complained Sue, with magnificent scorn. "What have old ivy leaves to do with your getting well? And you used to love that vine so, you naughty girl! Don't be a goosey. Why, the doctor told me this morning that your chances for getting well real soon were—let's see exactly what he said—he said the chances were ten to one! Why, that's almost as good a chance as we have in New York when we ride on the street cars or walk past a new building. Try to take some broth now, and let Sudie go back to her drawing, so she can sell the editor man with it, and buy port wine for her sick child, and pork chops for her greedy self."

"You needn't get any more wine", said Johnsy, keeping her eyes fixed out the window. "There goes another. No, I don't want any broth. That leaves just four. I want to see the last one fall before it gets dark. Then I'll go, too."

"Johnsy, dear", said Sue, bending over her, "will you promise me to keep your eyes closed, and not look out the window until I am done working? I must hand those drawings in by to-morrow. I need the light, or I would draw the shade soon."

"Couldn't you draw in the other room?" asked Johnsy, coldly.

"I'd rather be here by you", said Sue. "Besides, I don't want you to keep looking at those silly ivy leaves."

"Tell me as soon as you have finished", said Johnsy, closing her eyes, and lying white and still as a fallen statue, "because I want to see the last one fall. I'm tired of waiting. I'm tired of thinking. I want to turn loose my

192

go: (from this world), die; be gone, be dead; far gone, terminally ill, about to die.

nonsense: rubbish; nonsensical, absurd □ **complained:** protested

scorn: disdain, contempt □ **...to do...:** what is the connexion between leaves and your recovery? □ **so:** (Am.) so much

naughty girl!: bad girl! □ **goose(y):** stupid person □ **why:** (here) expresses protest (≠ why?) □ **real soon:** (Am.) really soon, in very little time; it's real good!

ten to one: the banks give you ten francs *to* the dollar

ride: go by bus, by train, in a car, on horseback... □ **street car(s):** (Am.) tram-car □ **new:** (here) being built □ **broth:** a kind of soup

so she can sell: (Am.) so that...

editor: one who controls a newspaper □ **sick:** ill, unwell

chop(s): pork chop, mutton chop, veal cutlet □ **greedy:** gluttonous

needn't: indicates absence of obligation (≠ must, have to)

there goes another: emphatic for "another (leaf) goes"

that leaves just four: only four (leaves) are left, remain on the ivy vine; leave, left, left; one leaf, two leaves

dark: it gets dark at five o'clock in the evening in winter

bending: you bend over your table when you write

closed: shut

I am done working: I have finished working □ **hand... in:** give to the editor □ **light:** the sun gives light (≠ darkness)

draw the shade: close the shade (≠ pull up); shade (Am.) blind, store

draw: notice the two meanings of "draw"

coldly: in an unfriendly way, unkindly

I'd rather be: I prefer to be □ **by:** near □ **besides:** in addition, moreover □ **keep (on) looking:** continue, go on looking

as soon as you have...: immediately after you have (present!)

still: without movement, motionless; keep still! Stop moving!

I'm tired of...: I've had enough of, I'm fed up with + ing

turn loose: relax (≠ reinforce); loose ≠ firm, tight.

hold on everything, and go sailing down, down, just like one of those poor, tired leaves".

"Try to sleep", said Sue. "I must call Behrman up to be my model for the old hermit miner. I'll not be gone a minute. Don't try to move until I come back."

Old Behrman was a painter who lived on the ground floor beneath them. He was past sixty and had a Michael Angelo's Moses beard curling down from the head of a satyr along the body of an imp. Behrman was a failure in
10 art. Forty years he had wielded the brush without getting near enough to touch the hem of his Mistress's robe. He had been always about to paint a masterpiece, but had never yet begun it. For several years he had painted nothing except now and then a daub in the line of commerce or advertising. He earned a little by serving as a model to those young artists in the colony who could not pay the price of a professional. He drank gin to excess, and still talked of his coming masterpiece. For the rest he was a fierce little old man, who scoffed terribly at softness in any
20 one, and who regarded himself as especial mastiff-in-waiting to protect the two young artists in the studio above.

Sue found Behrman smelling strongly of juniper berries in his dimly lighted den below. In one corner was a blank canvas on an easel that had been waiting there for twenty-five years to receive the first line of the masterpiece. She told him of Johnsy's fancy, and how she feared she would, indeed, light and fragile as a leaf herself, float away, when her slight hold upon the world grew weaker.
30 Old Behrman, with his red eyes plainly streaming shouted his contempt and derision for such idiotic imaginings.

194

hold: act of holding (on to everything, to life) □ **sailing:** going like a boat in the wind (without any effort or interest)

call... up: go and see him and ask him to come

model: one who sits for a painter □ **miner:** man working in a mine

until: (one l!), till (two l's!)

ground floor: floor of a building nearest to the ground

beneath: under □ **past sixty:** over, more than sixty years old

beard: hair on the face □ **curling:** twisting (≠ straight); curls of hair

imp: demon, evil genius, little devil □ **failure:** person who fails (≠ succeeds) □ **wielded the brush without getting...:** used the brush (to paint with) without getting any success

about to: on the point of + ing □ **masterpiece:** piece of work (art, literature) which is the best of its type

now and then: from time to time □ **daub:** badly painted picture

advertising: publicity; advertise a product □ **earned:** earned money, made money (≠ win a competition, a game...)

to excess: exaggeratedly □ **still talked:** continued talking (≠ still, yet, however) □ **coming:** (masterpiece) to come

fierce: violent, rough □ **scoffed (at):** mocked (at) □ **softness:** feebleness, weakness (≠ strength) □ **mastiff:** large, strong dog used as a watchdog (to watch over, to protect people)

smelling of: note "of"! □ **juniper berries:** *baies de genièvre*

dimly lighted den below: almost dark...; dim ≠ bright; den (fam.), private room for study; below, downstairs □ **easel:** an easel supports a picture, a blackboard...

fancy: idea, opinion without foundation □ **feared:** was afraid

indeed: (here): certainly □ **light:** ≠ heavy □ **float:** move on the surface of water □ **slight:** insignificant □ **grew weaker:** became less strong □ **plainly:** evidently □ **streaming:** (with tears) crying □ **shouted his contempt:** expressed his contempt violently.

"Vass!" he cried. "Is dere people in de world mit der foolishness to die because leafs dey drop off from a confounded vine? I haf not heard of such a thing. No, I will not bose as a model for your fool hermit-dunderhead. Vy do you allow dot silly pusiness to come in der prain of her? Ach, dot poor leetle Miss Yohnsy."

"She is very ill and weak", said Sue, "and the fever has left her mind morbid and full of strange fancies. Very well, Mr. Behrman, if you do not care to pose for me, you
10 needn't. But I think you are a horrid old—old flibberti-gibbet."

"You are just like a woman!" yelled Behrman. "Who said I will not bose? Go on. I come mit you. For half an hour I haf peen trying to say dot I am ready to bose. Gott! dis is not any blace in which one so goot as Miss Johnsy shall lie sick. Some day I vill baint a masterpiece, and ve shall all go away. Gott! yes."

Johnsy was sleeping when they went upstairs. Sue pulled the shade down to the window-sill, and motioned
20 Behrman into the other room. In there they peered out the window fearfully at the ivy vine. Then they looked at each other for a moment without speaking. A persistent, cold rain was falling, mingled with snow. Behrman, in his old blue shirt, took his seat as the hermit-miner on an upturned kettle for a rock.

When Sue awoke from an hour's sleep the next morning she found Johnsy with dull, wide-open eyes staring at the drawn green shade.

"Pull it up; I want to see", she ordered, in a whisper.
30 Wearily Sue obeyed.

But, lo! after the beating rain and fierce gusts of wind that had endured through the livelong night, there yet stood out

196

"vass!": German for "what!" □ **is dere...:** are there... the... with...

foolishness: stupidity □ **drop off:** fall off

confounded: damned, wretched; he's a confounded fool!

fool: (for foolish) a fool is a foolish, stupid person

dunderhead: stupid person □ **vy...:** why do you permit that silly business (idea) to enter her head? □ **prain:** bad pronunciation of "brain" (mind, intellect) □ **fever:** temperature; have a fever, have a temperature □ **strange:** odd, bizarre

if you do not care to: if you do not want to □ **pose:** sit as a model for a painter □ **flibbertigibbet:** silly person who talks too much, changes her mind often

yelled: shouted, screamed, hollered; don't yell at me, I'm doing the best I can! □ **half an hour:** also: a quarter of an hour, an hour and a half (position of "a", "an")

dis is not any blace: in good English: this is no place

lie: lie, lay, lain; Miss Johnsy is lying on her bed (≠ lay, laid, laid; he laid the knife on the table)

window-sill: shelf below a window □ **motioned:** motioned him to enter with a gesture of the hand □ **peered:** looked closely as if unable to see well □ **fearfully:** with fear or fright; fearful (one l!), full of fear (≠ fearless)

mingled with: mixed with; he mingles with all sorts of people

took his seat: sat down; seat: chair, armchair... □ **upturned:** having been turned over □ **kettle:** for boiling water in

awoke: stopped sleeping, woke up □ **an hour's sleep:** an hour's walk, a mile's walk... □ **dull:** ≠ bright □ **staring:** looking fixedly (at) with wide open eyes

ordered: asked, commanded, demanded (≠ order a drink in a pub)

wearily: weary, tired in body and mind □ **obeyed:** obey (sb.)

lo!: (old use) look! □ **gust(s):** sudden strong rush of wind

endured: gone on, lasted □ **livelong:** whole, entire, complete

197

against the brick wall one ivy leaf. It was the last one on the vine. Still dark green near its stem, but with its serrated edges tinted with the yellow of dissolution and decay, it hung bravely from a branch some twenty feet above the ground.

"It is the last one", said Johnsy. "I thought it would surely fall during the night. I heard the wind. It will fall to-day, and I shall die at the same time."

"Dear, dear!" said Sue, leaning her worn face down to
10 the pillow, "think of me, if you won't think of yourself? What would I do?"

But Johnsy did not answer. The lonesomest thing in all the world is a soul when it is making ready to go on its mysterious, far journey. The fancy seemed to possess her more strongly as one by one the ties that bound her to friendship and to earth were loosed.

The day wore away, and even through the twilight they could see the lone ivy leaf clinging to its stem against the wall. And then, with the coming of the night
20 the north wind was again loosed, while the rain still beat against the windows and pattered down from the low Dutch eaves.

When it was light enough Johnsy, the merciless, commanded that the shade be raised.

The ivy leaf was still there.

Johnsy lay for a long time looking at it. And then she called to Sue, who was stirring her chicken broth over the gas stove.

"I've been a bad girl, Sudie", said Johnsy. "Something
30 has made that last leaf stay there to show me how wicked I was. It is a sin to want to die. You may bring me a little broth now, and some milk with a little port in it, and—no,

198

... stood out against: was easily seen against (the wall)
dark green: ≠ light green □ **stem:** *tige* □ **serrated:** *dentelé*
edge(s): border □ **tinted with:** coloured with □ **decay:** decomposition, rot □ **hung:** hang, hung, hung □ **some:** some twenty feet, about twenty feet, twenty feet or thereabouts.

surely: certainly, no doubt, undoubtedly
at the same time... as the leaf: note: same *as,* other *than*
leaning...: bending and lying her face... □ **worn:** tired, exhausted
pillow: cushion for your head (on bed) □ **think of:** prepositions are always difficult!
the lonesomest: lonesome, sad because alone, lonely
soul: (here) human being; there wasn't a soul in the street
far journey: expedition, travel to distant places (here, death)
tie(s): (sth.) that unites; family ties □ **bound:** attached, tied
earth: the planet we live on □ **loosed:** made loose (≠ firm, tight)
wore away: passed slowly □ **twilight:** half light just before nightfall
lone: solitary □ **clinging to:** holding on to

loosed: unchained (like a dog)
beat: beat, beat, beaten □ **pattered:** made tapping sound
eaves: edges of a roof coming out beyond walls
merciless: cruel, pitiless
be raised: should be raised, pulled up
still: still (continuation); again, always (repetition)

stirring: moving a spoon (in her soup) □ **chicken:** young bird, especially young hen □ **gas stove:** gas cooker

stay: remain □ **to show:** in order to show □ **wicked:** very bad
sin: offence against God; a sinner is one who commits a sin, he sins against God; a sinful action

bring me a hand-mirror first, and then pack some pillows about me, and I will sit up and watch you cook."

An hour later she said:

"Sudie, some day I hope to paint the Bay of Naples."

The doctor came in the afternoon, and Sue had an excuse to go into the hallway as he left.

"Even chances", said the doctor, taking Sue's thin, shaking hand in his. "With good nursing you'll win. And now I must see another case I have downs-
10 tairs. Behrman, his name is—some kind of an artist, I believe. Pneumonia, too. He is an old, weak man, and the attack is acute. There is no hope for him; but he goes to the hospital to-day to be made more comfortable."

The next day the doctor said to Sue: "She's out of danger. You've won. Nutrition and care now—that's all".

And that afternoon Sue came to the bed where Johnsy lay, contentedly knitting a very blue and very useless woollen shoulder scarf, and put one arm around her,
20 pillows and all.

"I have something to tell you, white mouse", she said. "Mr. Behrman died of pneumonia to-day in the hospital. He was ill only two days. The janitor found him on the morning of the first day in his room downstairs helpless with pain. His shoes and clothing were wet through and icy cold. They couldn't imagine where he had been on such a dreadful night. And then they found a lantern, still lighted, and a ladder that had been dragged from its place, and some scattered brushes, and a palette
30 with green and yellow colors mixed on it, and—look out the window, dear, at the last ivy leaf on the wall. Didn't you wonder why it never fluttered or moved when the wind

first: to begin with □ **pack:** put together, gather
about me: round me □ **sit up:** sit up (in bed) from a lying position;
sit down (from a standing position); sit, be seated
I hope: I expect and desire...; hope; hopeful ≠ hopeless
in the afternoon: in the morning, in the evening (note "in")
as he left: when he left, on leaving
even chances: fifty fifty; even, equal; our score is even
shaking: trembling □ **nursing:** looking after (a hospital nurse),
taking care of □ **win:** win, won, won ≠ lose, lost, lost
some kind of an artist: an artist, sort of...
I believe: I think; I believe in God; religious belief
acute: severe, serious, at a peak

care: intensive care unit (in a hospital); the patient needs constant
care; "glass, handle with care"

knitting: making clothes with wool and long needles □ **useless:** of
no use (≠ useful) □ **woollen:** made of wool □ **scarf:** piece of cloth
worn round neck or over shoulders
white mouse: (here: term of endearment) my darling; cats and mice
(one mouse, two mice)
janitor: (Am.) person who takes care of a building, keeping it clean,
doing some repairs, caretaker
helpless with pain: suffering terribly □ **wet through:** very wet
(because of the rain), soaked through, drenched (≠ dry)
dreadful: unpleasant; what dreadful weather!
ladder: (sth.) used for climbing up walls □ **dragged:** pulled along
(with difficulty) □ **scattered:** put here and there
colors: (Am. spelling) colours; honor, labor, favor... (no u !)

wonder why: ask yourself why □ **fluttered:** trembled, shook

blew? Ah, darling, it's Behrman's masterpiece—he painted it there the night that the last leaf fell.

blew: blow, blew, blown; the wind is blowing hard
the night that the last leaf fell: or the night (when) the last leaf fell;
fall, fell, fallen

Grammaire au fil des nouvelles

Traduisez les phrases suivantes inspirées du texte (le premier chiffre renvoie aux pages, les suivants aux lignes) :

Est-elle tracassée par quelque chose qui vaille la peine qu'on y pense? (**some, any, no; be worth**+...; 188.15).

Je ferai *tout ce que* la science peut accomplir (188.21).

Si vous réussissez à la persuader de poser une seule question sur les modes d'hiver... (**get sb to**, 188.24).

Les jeunes artistes doivent se frayer un chemin vers *l'*Art *en dessinant* des illustrations pour des magazines (emploi de **the**, 190.4,5).

Il y a trois jours il y en avait presque cent (190.27).

Il n'en reste que cinq (structure avec **left**, 190.29).

Quand la dernière tombera il faudra que je m'en aille (**when, while, as soon as**+...; rôle de **one**, 190.32 et 192.1).

Qu'est-ce que des feuilles de lierre ont à voir avec le fait que tu te portes bien? (gérondif, 192.4).

Tu n'as plus besoin de prendre de vin (semi-modaux **need** et **dare**; quantité supplémentaire, 192.15).

J'aimerais mieux être près de toi. Je ne veux pas que tu *continues à regarder* ces feuilles (proposition infinitive, 192.27,28).

Je suis fatigué d'attendre (prépositions+gérondif, 192.32).

Le vieux Behrman était peintre (noms de personnes précédés d'un adjectif familier ou d'un titre, 194.6).

Johnsy *dormait* quand ils *montèrent* à l'étage supérieur (emploi des formes simple et continue, 196.18).

Elles se regardèrent un instant sans parler (réciprocité; prépositions suivies du gérondif, 196.21,22).

Sue se réveilla le lendemain matin après *une heure de sommeil* (notions de durée, de distance avec le génitif, 196.26).

Je veux voir (**want**+..., 196.29).

Vocabulaire en contexte

Voici 1700 mots rencontrés dans les nouvelles, suivis du sens qu'ils ont dans celles-ci.

— A —

a bit un peu
a good bit beaucoup
a trifle un peu
about au sujet de
above plus de
above au-dessus de
abroad à l'étranger
absently ne pensant à autre chose
absentmindedly distraitement
abstractedly d'un air rêveur, absent
account compte (courant...)
ache être douloureux, faire mal
acute aigu, sévère
adress écrire une adresse (sur enveloppe)
advertising publicité
advice conseils
afford pouvoir se payer
afoot en train, qui se prépare
agree with être d'accord avec
ahead of devant
air out aérer, sécher
airship dirigeable
airy désinvolte
aisle allée (entre deux rangs)
alike identique
all in all tout bien considéré
all the same quand même
allow autoriser
almond amande
almost presque
alone seul
aloud à haute voix
altogether en tout
amicable amical
among parmi
amount to se réduire à, revenir à
angrily avec colère
angry (with sb.) en colère (contre qqn)
answer répondre
anxiety envie

anxious to désireux, impatient de
anyway de toute façon
apologize s'excuser
applicant postulant, candidat
aquiline (d')aigle
arch arquer
arched voûté, cintré
area zone
arm bras
armchair fauteuil
armour blindage
artful rusé
as a matter of fact en fait
as soon as dès que
as though comme si
ashamed of (be) avoir honte de
aside de côté
ask to inviter à
asparagus asperges
assign (to) transférer (à)
astonishing étonnant
astound stupéfier
at ease à l'aise
at last enfin
at least au moins
at length enfin
attend to s'occuper de
average (on the) (en) moyenne
awake (ré)veillé
awake, awoke ou awaked, awoken réveiller
awe respect mêlé de crainte
awful affreux
awkward gênant

— B —

back aller à reculons
back arrière
back dos
backward(s) à reculons
bad mauvais
battleship cuirassé
ball-point pen stylo à bille

bare nu
bare simple, sans rien de plus
barely à peine
barn grange
basket panier
bathtub (am.) baignoire
beach plage
bead grain de chapelet
beard barbe
bear, bore, borne porter
beat, beat, beaten battre
beckon faire signe (à)
become, became, become devenir
bed and breakfast chambre avec
    petit déjeuner
bedclothes draps et couvertures
bedraggled détrempé, sali par la
    pluie
bedside chevet
bedspread couvre-lit
bedstead châlit, lit
beggar mendiant
beggar (little) (petit) coquin, frip-
    pon
begin, began, begun commencer
behold! voyez! voici!
Belgium Belgique
belief croyance
believe croire
bell cloche, sonnette
belly ventre
bell-button timbre (sonnette)
belong to appartenir à, relever de
belongings affaires
below sous
bench banc
bend, bent, bent se pencher
beneath sous
berry baie, fruit
beside à côté de
besides en outre
bet, bet ou betted, bet ou betted
    parier
bewilder égarer, abasourdir
beyond au-dessus de
beyond au-delà de
bid, bade ou bid, bidden ou bid
    dire (au revoir...)
bill facture
bill of fare menu
bind, bound, bound lier
bird oiseau

birth naissance
birthmark marque de naissance
bishop évêque
bishop sleeve manche à gigot
bit morceau
bitch putain
bite bouchée
bite, bit, bitten mordre
bitter amer
bitterly amèrement
blank nu (mur), vide
bleak morne, triste
blemish imperfection
blessing bénédiction
blind aveugle
blink cligner des yeux
bliss béatitude
block boucher, bloquer
block (am.) pâté de maisons
blood sang
bloodless exsangue
bloodshot injecté de sang
blot tache, pâté (d'encre)
blotch tacher
blotchy taché
blotter (desk) sous-main
blouse (am.) veste d'uniforme
blow away, blew, blown emporter,
    faire sauter
blow, blew, blown souffler
bluish bleuâtre
blush teinte rose
board planche
board (up) fermer au moyen de
    planches
boarding-house   pension   de
    famille
body corps
boldly hardiment
bookcase bibliothèque
boot gros soulier
boot botte
border frontière, limite
borrow sth from sb emprunter
    qqch à qqn
bosh! bêtises!
boss patron
bother se tracasser
bottle bouteille
bottom bas
bottom drawer dernier tiroir (du
    bas)

bow courbette
box up enfermer
box (letter box) boîte (aux lettres)
brain cerveau
branch filiale, succursale
break, broke, broken enfreindre (la loi)
breast pocket poche intérieure
breath souffle, haleine
breath souffle (vent)
breathe (on) respirer, (souffler sur)
breathlessly en haletant
bright vif (couleur), brillant
brighten se dérider
brightly d'un air radieux
bring oneself to do se résoudre à faire
bring up élever (enfant)
bring, brought, brought apporter
broad large
brokenly avec des interruptions
bronx cheer bruit de dérision
broth bouillon
brown brun
brownstone (house) grès de construction
brow, eyebrow sourcil
brush brosser
brush pinceau
build, built, built bâtir
burden charger, accabler
bur (écossais) ruisseau
burn, burnt, burnt brûler
burst into tears, burst, burst éclater en larmes
bursting plein à craquer
burst, burst, burst éclater
business affaire, société
business devoir, occupation
but sauf, excepté
buttonhole boutonnière
buy, bought, bought acheter
buzz bourdonner
buzzard buse
by près de

— C —

cab taxi
call téléphoner

call appel (téléphonique)
call appeler, nommer
call in faire venir, convoquer
canvas toile
can't help + ing ne pouvoir s'empêcher de
cap casquette
cap with coiffer de
car (Am.) wagon, voiture
care s'inquiéter
care for aimer
care to vouloir
carefully avec précaution
carriage voiture
carry porter
carry on continuer
casing enveloppe, revêtement
cask baril
castle château fort
casually en passant, fortuitement
catch sight of, caught, caught apercevoir
catch, caught, caught attraper, prendre
caution précaution
cellar cave
cement ciment
chafing-dish réchaud (de table)
change one's mind changer d'avis
chap type, homme
chap bajoue
charge demander (tel prix pour)
charge accusation
charity œuvre de bienfaisance
chat brin de causette
chatter caquetage, bavardage
chatter claquer des dents
cheap bon marché
check vérifier
checkup bilan de santé
cheek joue
cheekbone pommette
chest poitrine
chicken poulet
childhood enfance
chill froid
chilly frileux
chin menton
choice choix
choke étouffer
choose, chose, chosen choisir
choosy difficile

chop côtelette
Christmas Eve la veille de Noël
church église
citizen citoyen
clad vêtu
clamber grimper en s'aidant des pieds
clean propre
clean-shaven bien rasé
clear s'éclaircir (la voix...)
clench serrer
clever intelligent
climb grimper
cling, clung, clung se cramponner (à)
cloak manteau
close finir
close fermer
close près
closely étroitement, en serrant fort
clothes vêtements
clothe, clothed ou clad, clothed ou clad vêtir
clothing vêtements
cloud nuage
clutch empoigner
coarse grossier
cock one's eye at sb. cligner de l'œil à qqn
coldly avec froideur
collapse s'effondrer
collar col
collect aller chercher
collector collecteur, percepteur
comfortingly comme pour réconforter
coming à venir, futur
complacency satisfaction, contentement
complain se plaindre
compulsion contrainte
concern intérêt, souci
confide in se confier à
confounded fichu, sacré
confused déconcerté, troublé
congenial de la même nature
connect relier
consequence importance
contempt mépris
contemptible méprisable
contents contenu

cook cuisiner
copper cuivre rouge
copper flic
coppers la petite monnaie
cork bouchon
corpse cadavre
cost, cost, cost coûter
cot(tage) maisonnette
cough tousser
count compter
count on compter sur
cow vache
coward (y) poltron
cower se tapir
crack fissure
crack lézarder
craggy rocailleux
crash s'écraser
crate caisse à claire-voie
cream crème (couleur)
creep, crept, crept se glisser furtivement
cricketer joueur de cricket
crippled estropié, infirme
crisply de manière raide, apprêtée
crop couper court (cheveux)
cross traverser
cross croiser
cross between mélange (de... et de...)
cruiser croiseur
crumb miette
crumble tomber en ruine, en poussière
crush écraser
crutch béquille
cry pleurer
cubby-hole retraite, cachette, niche
cunning rusé
cup (one's hands) mettre ses mains en coupe
cupboard placard
curl friser
curl replier
curl up (se) pelotonner
curse malédiction
curtain rideau
custard crème anglaise
customary d'usage
cut back, cut, cut retourner
cut out, cut, cut supprimer

— D —

dachshund basset allemand
dainty affecté, maniéré, petit, délicat
damp humide
dank humide et froid
dare oser
dark sombre
dark green vert foncé
dark grey gris foncé
darkness obscurité
darts fléchettes
daub croûte (peinture)
daughter fille (par rapport aux parents)
daze étourdissement
deal with agir avec, traiter
deal with, dealt, dealt avoir affaire à
deal (a great) beaucoup
dear me! mon Dieu !
death la mort
debt dette
decay dépérir (plante)
decay pourriture, décomposition
deep profond
deeply profondément
deep-set enfoncé (yeux)
defect défaut
delight grand plaisir
delighted with enchanté de
delusion illusion
den antre, tanière
deny nier
deny oneself se priver
deny sb sth priver qqn de qqch
deserving méritant
desk bureau (meuble)
desk blotter sous-main
desk job travail de bureau
destroy détruire
devil (little) gredin (petit)
devious sinueux
dial composer (un numéro)
die mourir
dim obscur(ci)
dimly lighted faiblement éclairé
dip plonger qqch dans un liquide
dirt saleté
discomfort gêne, malaise
disgraceful honteux
disguise cacher
dish plat
dismal lugubre
dive plonger, se précipiter (vers)
do up, did, done retaper
dodge se jeter de côté, s'esquiver
dotty toqué
doubtful de doute
downstairs en bas
drag traîner (qqch de lourd)
drag oneself se traîner
draggle se crotter
draught courant d'air
draw oneself se redresser (fièrement)
drawer tiroir
drawing board planche à dessin
draw, drew, drawn (at) tirer
draw, drew, drawn dessiner
dreadfully terriblement, très
dream rêve
dreary lugubre
drink, drank, drunk boire
drip (faire) tomber goutte à goutte
drive rue, allée privée
driver conducteur
drop tomber
drop goutte
drown noyer
drug dealer trafiquant de drogue
drunkard ivrogne
drunken (d')ivrogne
dry sécher
dry sec
dull sans vie
dump décharger, déposer
dunderhead imbécile
dungarees combinaison
duty (on) de service

— E —

each chaque
ear oreille
early matinal
early de bonne heure
earn gagner (argent)
earth la terre
easel chevalet
eat, ate, eaten manger

209

eaves avancée (du toit)
edge (re)bord
effusive expansif
elder ancien
elderly assez vieux
else autre
embers braise, charbons ardents
empty vide
enclose mettre sous enveloppe, envoyer
end terminer
endure durer
entrance entrée
entry entrée
even même
even égal (voix), régulier
even though même si
expand déployer
expect s'attendre à
explain expliquer
extend s'étendre
extra supplémentaire
exultantly de manière triomphante
eyelid paupière

— F —

face faire face à
fade se faner, se flétrir, passer
fade away mourir (voix), disparaître
fail échouer
failure raté (personne)
faintly faiblement, légèrement
fair juste
fair and square en plein
fair game franc jeu
fall away dépérir
fall to doing, fell, fallen se mettre à (faire)
fall, fell, fallen tomber
false faux
fancy idée folle, fantaisie
fancy croire, s'imaginer
far lointain, éloigné
far too... beaucoup trop...
fashion manière
fast vite
fat gras, gros
fawn on sb flatter qqn servilement

fear craindre
fearfully avec crainte
features traits (du visage)
feebly faiblement
feed, fed, fed nourrir
feel, felt, felt (se) sentir, ressentir
fellow type, gars
field champ
fierce violent, brutal
fiercely d'un air féroce
fight combat, bagarre
fight, fought, fought se battre
figure silhouette
fill in remplir (formulaire)
fill with remplir de
filling plombage
find, found, found trouver
fine beau
fine (très) bien
finger doigt
fingernail ongle
finger-smudged avec des taches de doigt
finger-soiled avec des taches de doigt
fire feu
fish (du) poisson
fishing la pêche
fist poing
fit crise, accès
flake (s') écailler
flap rabat
flash briller, étinceler
flash éclair
fleshy chair (couleur)
flibbertigibbet tête de linotte
flight (of stairs) escalier
fling, flung, flung jeter violemment
flip donner une chiquenaude
float flotter
floor étage
flour farine
flourish brandir
fly mouche
fly, flew, flown aller en avion
fly, flew, flown passer vite (temps), voler
folk(s) gens
follow suivre
following suivant
fond of (be) aimer beaucoup

food nourriture
fool duper
foolishness stupidité
foot pied : 30, 48 cm
footstep (bruit de) pas
foot, feet pied
for instance par exemple
forbid, forbade, forbidden interdire
forefinger index
forehead front
foreigner étranger
forever à jamais
forget, forgot, forgotten oublier
forgive, forgave, forgiven pardonner
form formulaire
fortuneteller diseuse de bonne aventure
forward en avant, vers l'avant
fourth quart
frail fragile
frame cadre
free libre
free of libéré de
fresh nouveau, non usagé
friendship amitié
frighten effrayer
frisky fringant
front door porte sur rue
front leg patte de devant
fulfil réaliser (promesse)
full complet, plein
funeral enterrement
funeral procession convoi funèbre
funny étrange
fur fourrure
furnished meublé
fuss about s'affairer

— G —

garment vêtement
gas gazer
gas fire appareil de chauffage au gaz
gasp haleter
gas-ring réchaud à gaz (à un feu)
gate portail
gather se rassembler
gaunt décharné

genteel distingué
gentle doux
gently doucement
gesture geste
get dark, got, got faire noir
get down to en arriver à
get off, got, got quitter
get over, got, got se remettre de
get up, got, got se lever
get well, got, got se porter bien
get, got, got zigouiller, tuer
ghost fantôme
give onself away se trahir
give up abandonner
glad content
glance at jeter un coup d'œil sur
glare at jeter un regard de colère à
glasses lunettes
glitter briller (de convoitise...)
glove gant
glow rougeoyer
glower lancer des regards mauvais
go wrong aller mal
God damn it! nom de Dieu !
gold or
gold-rimmed aux montures en or
good (du) bien
good gracious me ! mon Dieu !
goose (y) nigaud
gossip faire des commérages
grab empoigner
grand piano piano à queue
grannie mamie
grateful reconnaissant
gravelly graveleux, mêlé de gravier
gray (am.) gris
great grand
greedy gourmand
greenstuff légumes verts
greenhouse serre
greet saluer
greetings salutations, vœux
grey-haired aux cheveux gris
grief chagrin
grim lugubre
grimly d'un air ou d'un ton sinistre
grinding oppressant, écrasant
grizzled grisonnant

211

groan gémir
groceries articles d'épicerie
ground sol
ground floor rez-de-chaussée
grounds enceinte (d'un hôpital..)
grow, grew, grown pousser, croître
grow up, grew, grown pousser, grandir, devenir adulte
grow + adj, grew, grown devenir
gruffly d'un ton bourru
guarled noueux
guess deviner, supposer
guest client (d'un hôtel), pensionnaire
guest invité
gust rafale

— H —

habit habitude
hack hacher, couper
hair poil
hale tirer avec force
half way up à mi-hauteur (de)
half-crown demi-couronne (pièce) (2 shillings et 6 pence)
half-darkness semi-obscurité
half-way à mi-chemin
hallway vestibule
hamper panier d'osier
hand tendre, passer
handkerchief mouchoir
handsome élégant
hand-mirror glace à main
hang around flâner, traîner
hang up (Am.), hung, hung raccrocher (téléphone)
hangar hangar (pour avions)
hang, hung, hung (sus) pendre
happen arriver (événement)
happen to do se trouver à faire (par hasard)
hard fermement
harden durcir
hardly à peine
harm mal
harmless inoffensif
hastily à la hâte
hate haine
hate détester

haze (légère) vapeur
head chef, leader
head waiter maître d'hôtel
headline titre, manchette (des journaux)
headquarters siège (de société)
headquarters bureau central
heap entasser
heart milieu
hearth âtre
heartless sans cœur
hear, heard, heard entendre
heating chauffage
heave, heaved ou hove, heaved (sou)lever
heavy lourd
helm barre, gouvernail
help aide
help! au secours!
helpless désespéré
helpless impuissant, désarmé
hem bord, ourlet
hick donner des coups de pied à
hide, hid, hidden cacher
hide, hid, hidden se cacher
highway grand-route
hoard trésor (amassé)
hold prise
hold on conserver (téléphone)
hold, held, held (re)tenir
hole trou
holster étui (de revolver)
hope espérer
horseshow concours hippique
hospitable hospitalier, accueillant
hot (trop) fort (plaisanterie)
huddle (up) se blottir
huge immense, énorme
hungry (be) avoir faim
Huns Boches
hunt for être à la chasse de
hurl jeter violemment
hurry (up) se dépêcher
hurt, hurt, hurt faire mal à
husband mari

— I —

icy glacial
ignore feindre d'ignorer
ill malade

212

imbalance déséquilibre
imp diablotin, petit démon
inadequate insuffisant
inarticulate mal prononcé
incomer nouveau venu, intrus
incorporated constitué en société
    commerciale
indeed en vérité, vraiment
ingratiating insinuant, doucereux
ink encre
inland à l'intérieur des terres
inside à l'intérieur
instead of au lieu de
interfere (with) se mêler (de)
interval entr'acte
iron fer
iron-barred aux barres de fer
irrelevantly hors de propos
ivy lierre

— J —

jab coup de poing, coup sec
jack-in-the box diable à ressort
jail prison
jam-pot pot à confiture
janitor (Am.) concierge, gardien
Japanese Japonais
jerk secouer, donner une secousse
jersey tricot (vêtement)
joint (en) commun
jokingly en plaisantant
journey voyage
jump (sur) sauter
juniper genièvre

— K —

keep at, kept, kept persévérer dans
keep doing, kept, kept ne cesser de
    (faire)
keep, kept, kept tenir, garder
keep, kept, kept entretenir
kettle bouilloire
key clef
kick out chasser à coups de pied
kid gosse, enfant
kill tuer
kind sorte
kind bon, gentil, bienveillant

kind (your) les gens de ton espèce
kindergarten jardin d'enfants
kindness gentillesse
knee genou
knit, knit ou knitted tricoter
know, knew, known savoir

— L —

lace-curtained aux rideaux de
    dentelle
lack manque
ladder échelle
land pays
landing palier
landlady logeuse
landscape paysage
lane chemin creux
lapse (re)tomber (dans le
    silence...)
large grand
last fin, bout
last dernier
last durer
late tardif
lately récemment
later on plus tard
laughter rire
laundry linge (à laver)
law loi
lawful conforme à la loi
lazily paresseusement
lead, led, led conduire (à)
leaf, leaves feuille
lean maigre
lean, leant ou leaned, leant ou
    leaned se pencher
leap, leapt ou leaped, leapt ou
    leaped bondir
learn, learnt ou learned, learnt ou
    learned apprendre
leather cuir
leave permission (armée)
leave, left, left laisser, quitter
left gauche
leg pied (de meuble)
leg patte
length longueur
lens lentille
level plat
liar menteur

library bibliothèque
lick lécher
lid couvercle
lie mentir
lie mensonge
lie, lay, lain être couché
lift (sou)lever
light léger
lightly légèrement
light, lit ou lighted, lit ou lighted allumer
like quoi, hein
likely probablement, vraisemblablement
liking goût
limb membre
line up (Am.) faire la queue
linger traîner, rester longtemps
lining doublure
lip lèvre
livelong entier
loaf miche (de pain)
lodging logement
loll se prélasser
lone isolé, solitaire
lonesome seul, esseulé
long désirer ardemment
longing désir ardent
look air, mine
look sembler
look after s'occuper de
look for chercher
look forward to + ing attendre avec impatience
look here! écoutez !
look sharp! remuez-vous !
loose lâche, défait
loose ample
lose, lost, lost perdre
loss perte
low vil
lower baisser
luck chance
lucky chanceux
luncheon déjeuner
luncheonette restaurant *fast food*
lung poumon
lurk se cacher (menaçant)
lustrous brillant

— M —

madly comme un fou
maiden (sisters) (sœurs) célibataires
mail courrier
mail poster
mailboat bateau postal
mailbox (Am.) boîte aux lettres
main principal
major se spécialiser (à l'université)
make a note prendre note
make out, made, made distinguer
make up one's mind décider
manage se débrouiller
manage to réussir à
map carte (géographique)
maple érable
marvel merveille
mass panic panique générale
masterpiece chef-d'œuvre
mastiff (-in-waiting) gros chien de garde
match allumette
material tissu
matter question, problème
mayor maire
maze dédale
meal repas
mean mesquin, près de ses sous
meaning sens, signification
meaninglessly d'une manière dépourvue de sens
means moyens (financiers)
means (by all) absolument
mean, meant, meant vouloir, avoir l'intention
meat viande
meddlesome qui fourre son nez partout
medicine médicament
meet, met, met rencontrer
meet, met, met faire la connaissance de
melt fondre
merciless sans pitié
mere simple, pur et simple
middle-aged d'un certain âge, entre deux âges
midnight minuit
might pouvoir, moyens

mighty très
mile 1,609 kilomètre
mill moulin
mind esprit
mind avoir qqch contre
mind (have a good) avoir bien envie (de)
mind + ing voir un inconvénient à
mingle with mêler à
minister ministre (du culte, protestant)
mislay, mislaid, mislaid égarer
miss manquer (train)
missing disparu
mistake se méprendre sur
mistake faute, erreur
mite (of a woman) petit bout de femme
moon lune
Moses Moïse
mosquito moustique
moss-grown couvert de mousse
most la plupart de
mostly le plus souvent, principalement
motion faire signe (à)
mournful lugubre
mouse, mice souris
mouth bouche
mouth entrée
mouthful bouchée
move mouvement
move se déplacer
mud boue
muddy boueux
mug grande tasse sans soucoupe, chope
murderous épouvantable
mustard gas gaz moutarde
mutter marmonner

— N —

napkin serviette de table
narrow étroit
native autochtone
naughty méchant, vilain
navy la marine
navy-blue bleu marine
nearly presque

neat net, propre
neatly soigneusement
neck cou
need besoin
needlework ouvrage à l'aiguille
needy nécessiteux
neighbour voisin
nervous break down dépression nerveuse
nest nid
news nouvelles
next ensuite, après
next suivant, voisin
next morning (the) le lendemain matin
next to à côté de
night-shirt chemise de nuit
nod faire un signe de tête affirmatif
nonsense sottises
noodle (Am.) tronche, tête
northern du nord
nose museau
nostril narine
nothingness néant
notice écriteau
notice remarquer
notorious notoire
now and again de temps en temps
now and then de temps à autre
nowadays de nos jours
nuisance (personne) fléau, peste
numb engourdi
numerous nombreux
nun religieuse
nurse soigner
nutty savoureux

— O —

oak tree chêne
obey sb. obéir à qqn
obvious apparent, évident
occur to sb. venir à l'esprit de qqn
odd bizarre
offerings offrandes
off-chance chance improbable
old-fashioned d'autrefois, démodé
on the other hand d'autre part
on top of that par-dessus le marché

once jadis
only seul, unique
ooze suinter
open wide grand ouvert
order ordonner
order commander (un repas...)
outburst emportement, éclat
outlying éloigné, isolé
outside extérieur
outside en dehors
outside devant, en face de
outside hors de, à l'extérieur de
outsider étranger
over au-dessus de
over plus de
over au sujet de
over and done with fini pour de bon
overalls salopette
overcoat pardessus
overcome, overcame, overcome vaincre
overload surcharger
overlook donner sur (fenêtre)
overseas outremer
owing to en raison
own propre, personnel
owner propriétaire

— P —

pack entasser
package (Am.) paquet
pad aller à pas feutrés
padlock cadenas
pageant spectacle somptueux, grande fête
paint peinture
paint peindre
palate palais
palm paume (de la main)
pan casserole, poêlon
pane carreau
pantomime spectacle traditionnel de Noël en G.B.
paper-knife coupe-papier
parcel colis
parish paroisse
parlour petit salon
part se séparer
particular difficile, exigeant

pass laissez-passer, sauf-conduit
pass away disparaître, mourir
passer-by passant
pasteboard carton
pat tapoter
pat caresser
patch tache, marque
path allée (jardin)
patter tambouriner (pluie)
pattern motif
pave one's way se frayer un chemin
pavement trottoir
pay, paid, paid payer
peace paix
peach pêche
peacok paon
peck at donner des coups de bec à
peculiar étrange
peculiarly particulièrement, singulièrement
peel s'écailler
peer scruter
peg patère
pen plume
pence pluriel de penny
people des gens
pet animal familier
pick choisir
pick voler à la tire
pick up prendre, ramasser
pick up the phone décrocher le téléphone
pickle pétrin, difficulté
pickle conserver dans la saumure
picture tableau
piece morceau
piece pièce de monnaie
pike pique, pointe
pile empiler
pillar pilier
pillow oreiller
pinch pincée
pineapple ananas
pink rose (couleur)
pipe parler d'une voix flûtée
pit fosse
pitch-black noir comme de la poix
pity avoir pitié
plague fléau
plain évident

plainly de toute évidence
plane avion
please sb faire plaisir à
plenty of beaucoup de
plumbing installation sanitaire
plump dodu
plump (down) tomber lourdement
poke fourrer
pole poteau
pond étang
pop entrer ou sortir subitement
pop passer rapidement voir qqn
port (wine) porto
positively absolument
post poteau, pilier
postage port, affranchissement
pot (teapot) théière
pound livre (sterling) (100 pence)
pour verser
powder poudre
power puissance (pays)
power pouvoir
powerful puissant
pram landau
prattle jacasser
prayer prière
premises lieux
presently sous peu
preserve conserver
press harceler, talonner
pretty joli
pretty passablement, assez
price prix
priest prêtre
primordial premier, originel
print imprimer
probe explorer, sonder
proceed continuer
proceedings faits, actes
process processus
produce exhiber, montrer
promise perspective
protect (from) protéger de
proud of fier de
prowl rôder
puff bouffée, souffle
pull tirer
pull oneself together se reprendre
pull (in) entrer en gare
pulpit chaire
purpose but
push pousser

put, put, put dire, formuler
put away, put, put ranger
put on, put, put mettre (vêtements)
put out, put, put tendre (la main)
put up with, put, put supporter
puzzle (one's head) se creuser la tête

— Q —

quaint pittoresque, suranné
quaver chevroter (voix)
queer étrange
query s'enquérir
question doute
quite tout à fait
quiver tremblement, battement (paupière)
quiver trembler

— R —

rabbit lapin
radiance éclat, splendeur
radiant radieux
rag haillon
railroad (Am.) chemin de fer
rainy day (fig.) jour difficile, de disette
raise (sou)lever
randomly au hasard
rasher of bacon tranche de bacon
rate (at any) en tout cas
ravager dévastateur
raw brut, non traité
reach allonger la main
reach atteindre
read, read, read lire
realize se rendre compte
rear élever (enfants)
reckless insensé, imprudent
record archive
recover (from) se remettre (de)
refill remplir de nouveau
regard oneself as se considérer comme
rein rêne
relief soulagement
relieve soulager

remark dire, observer
remark observation, réflexion
remind sb. of sth. rappeler qqch à qqn
remote isolé
reply répondre
report signaler (à la police)
report to se présenter à (pour un travail)
repulsive rebutant
rest repos
rest se poser (yeux)
rest demeurer, rester
retort rétorquer
return rendre
rib côte (corps)
ride, rode, ridden aller (en bus, tramway...)
riding trousers pantalons de cheval
rifle fusil
right en plein
right approprié
right exact, juste
right coup du droit (poing)
right away immédiatement
rim bord
ring coup de sonnette
ring cercle
ring son
ring, rang, rung sonner
rip arracher, déchirer
ripple ride (sur l'eau)
rise, rose, risen se lever
rocker (off one's) toqué
roll (se) rouler
roof toit
rooming house (Am.) meublé, pension de famille
root racine
ropes ficelles (du métier)
rosy rosé, vermeil
rot balivernes
rub frotter
run promenade, tour
run, ran, run courir
rush se précipiter
rush élan, mouvement précipité
rust rouiller
rust rouille

sad triste
safe sûr, hors de danger
sail voguer, aller à la voile
sail aller d'un air conquérant
sand sable
sane sain (d'esprit)
saucer soucoupe
sausage saucisse
save sauver
say, said, said dire
scarcely à peine
scarf écharpe
scarlet écarlate
scatter éparpiller
schooling enseignement, instruction
scoff at se moquer de
score vingtaine
scorn dédain
scoundrel scélérat
scrape racler
scraping (bowing and) salamalecs
scream s'écrier
scrimp économiser sou par sou
seaman matelot
search fouiller
search recherche
searchlight projecteur
season saison
seat siège
seek, sought, sought chercher
seem sembler
see, saw, seen voir
seize saisir
self-confident sûr de soi
sell retail, sold, sold vendre au détail
sell, sold, sold vendre
sender expéditeur
send, sent, sent envoyer
service arme (armée, marine, air)
service (on) au service de qqn (comme servante)
set back from à l'écart de
set off for, set, set partir pour
set, set, set poser
set to mettre à (faire)
settle régler (compte, question)
settle s'établir, se fixer
several plusieurs

shabby mal mis, mal vêtu
shabby élimé
shabby minable
shade (Am.) store
shady ombragé
shaggy poilu, velu
shake hands with, shook, shaken serrer la main de
shake one's head, shook, shaken faire un signe de tête négatif
shake, shook, shaken trembler
shake, shook, shaken secouer
shame honte
shaped like en forme de
sharply sèchement
shed remise
sheep mouton
sheet feuille (de papier)
sheet drap
shelf étagère
shell obus
shine, shone, shone briller
shoe soulier
shoot down, shot, shot abattre (d'un coup de fusil)
shopkeeper marchand
short-breathed au souffle court
shoulder épaule
shoulder scarf châle
shout crier
show, showed, shown se voir
shrivel ratatiner
shrug hausser (les épaules)
shuffle traîner les pieds
shut, shut, shut (se) fermer
sick malade
side paroi
sigh soupirer
sight vue, spectacle
silver argent
simper sourire niaisement, minauder
sin péché
since depuis que
since étant donné que
single seul et unique
sing, sang, sung chanter
sink, sank, sunk s'enfoncer
sink, sank, sunk s'effondrer
sink, sank, sunk couler
sip boire à petite gorgée
sip petite gorgée

sit down, sat, sat s'asseoir
sit up, sat, sat rester debout, ne pas se coucher
sitting-room salon
sit, sat, sat être assis
sizzle grésiller
skeleton squelette
sketch esquisser, ébaucher
sky ciel
slam faire claquer (la porte)
slave peiner, travailler comme un esclave
sleep, slept, slept dormir
sleeve manche (vêtement)
slight léger, peu considérable
slightly légèrement
slim svelte
slimy vaseux, gluant
slipper pantoufle
slippery glissant
slot fente
slouch marcher lourdement
slowly lentement
smallpox variole
smash écraser, fracasser
smell odeur
smell of, smelt ou smelled, smelt ou smelled sentir
smile sourire
smile at sourire à
smite, smote, smitten frapper, détruire
smudge tache
snack casse-croûte
sneak away s'en aller furtivement
sniff renifler, flairer
snore ronfler, ronflement
snort renâcler, grogner
so to speak pour ainsi dire
soak tremper
sodden détrempé
soft mou, flasque
softly doucement
softness mollesse, faiblesse
soil tacher
solicitously avec sollicitude
some quelque (environ)
somehow d'une manière ou d'une autre
somewhat quelque peu, plutôt
son fils
song chanson

soon bientôt
sore pénible
soul âme
sound son
sound en bon état
sound sembler (à entendre)
spare se passer de
spare (to) de trop, en surplus
speech langage, parole(s)
spend, spend, spent dépenser
spend, spent, spent passer (du temps)
spitefully avec malveillance
splutter crachoter
splutter bredouiller
spoil, spoilt ou spoiled gâter
spook fantôme
spoonful cuillerée
spot repérer
spread, spread, spread (s')étaler
spring printemps
spring, sprang, sprung présenter brusquement (nouvelle)
sprinkle asperger, saupoudrer
spy apercevoir
spy on sb. espionner qqn
squarish plutôt carré
squat(ty) trapu
squelch faire flic flac
stage stade, étape
stair marche (d'escalier)
stair-rail rampe (d'escalier)
stalk marcher fièrement
stamp timbre
stand out against, stood, stood se détacher sur
stand, stood, stood se tenir (debout)
staple crampon à deux pointes
start over recommencer
start (up) sursauter
startle effrayer
starve mourir de faim
stately majestueux
stay séjourner, rester
steady ferme, solide
steal, stole, stolen voler (dérober)
steamy fumant
steel acier
stem tige
step marche (d'escalier)
step faire un pas

step back reculer
stick out, stuck, stuck saillir
stick, stuck, stuck coller
stick, stuck, stuck fourrer, mettre
stiffly avec raideur
still immobile
still encore (continuation)
stir (faire) bouger
stocks valeurs (en bourse)
stone 14 pounds = 6,35 kg
stop boucher
store entreposer
storm orage
story (Am.) étage
stout gros, corpulent
stove fourneau, poêle
straggling épars
straight droit, raide (cheveux)
straight tout droit, directement
straighten oneself se redresser
strange inconnu
strange bed lit qui n'est pas le sien
stranger inconnu
stream couler à flots
street car (Am.) tramway
street-lamp lampadaire
strength force
stretch étendre
stride, strode, stridden marcher à grands pas
strike a match, struck, struck ou stricken craquer une allumette
strike, struck, struck ou stricken frapper
string ficelle
strip bande
strong fort
strongly fortement
struggle se débattre
studio atelier (de peintre)
study étudier
stuff chose, truc
stuff empailler
stun abasourdir
sturdy solide
subdued doux (couleur), discret, effacé
subscribe to adhérer à, s'abonner à
substract soustraire
subway (Am.) métro

220

succeed (in doing) réussir (à faire)
suit costume
sullenly d'un air maussade
summer été
sunburned bronzé
sunflower tournesol
sunny ensoleillé
sunshiny ensoleillé
support (means of) (moyens de) subsistance
surmise supposer
surrender se rendre, abandonner
survey embrasser du regard
suspiciously avec méfiance
swagger se pavaner
swallow avaler
swamped with submergé de
sway se balancer
swear, swore, sworn jurer
sweat exploiter
sweaty moite de sueur (sweat)
sweet odorant
sweet adorable
swiftly rapidement
swim, swam, swum nager
swing, swung, swung se balancer, osciller
switch on allumer
swoop piquer, fondre sur

— T —

take advantage of avoir l'avantage sur, profiter de
take care of, took, taken prendre soin de
take hold, took, taken prendre appui
take one's life se suicider
take over, took, taken prendre la relève
take sth. to sb. porter qqch à qqn
tale histoire
talkative bavard
tall grand, élevé
tamper with falsifier
tantalizing torturant, qui met au supplice
tap tapoter
tar goudron
task (take sb. to) réprimander

taste goût
taste of avoir le goût de
taunt raillerie
teach, taught, taught enseigner
tear larme
tease taquiner
tea-tray plateau à thé
tedious ennuyeux
tell oneself, told, told se dire
tell, told, told dire
tenant locataire
test tester
thankful reconnaissant
thankless ingrat
the least le moindre
therapist (psycho) thérapeute
therefore en conséquence
thick épais
thief voleur
thin s'éclaircir, s'amenuiser
thin mince
think over, thought, thought repenser, réfléchir
third troisième
thoroughly minutieusement, à fond
threshold seuil
throat gorge
thought pensée
throw, threw, thrown jeter, lancer
thumb pouce
tickle chatouiller
tidy propre, bien rangé
tie lien
tight étanche
tilt incliner
tin boîte de conserve
tint with teinter de
tiny (tout) petit
tiny bit (a) un tout petit peu
tip bout
tip pourboire
tired of (+ ing) fatigué de
toe doigt de pied
together ensemble
tongue langue
top sommet
toss off avaler d'un trait
tough rude
tough dur
tour visiter, faire le tour d'un pays
towards vers

221

trade faire le commerce de
trade on (fig.) abuser de
tramp vagabond
travel voyager
tread, trod, trodden marcher (sur), fouler
trilby hat (chapeau) feutre
Trojan Troyen
trouble prendre la peine
trouble ennui, difficulté
truck (Am.) camion
true vrai
try essayer
tuck fourrer, enfoncer
tumbler verre sans pied
turd merde
turn away from se détourner de
turn back retourner
turn over retourner (qqch)
turtle tortue
twang accent nasillard
twice deux fois
twilight crépuscule
twirl tordre, tortiller
twist tordre, torsader
twitch se contracter nerveusement
tyre pneu

— U —

unable to incapable de
unarmed désarmé, dépourvu d'armes
unblemished sans défaut
undergraduate étudiant (non diplômé)
underlip lèvre inférieure
underneath sous
understand, understood, understood comprendre
undertaker entrepreneur des pompes funèbres
uneasiness malaise, gêne
uneasy mal à l'aise
unfed mal nourri
unfortunate malheureux
unfortunately malheureusement
ungrateful ingrat
unkind to désobligeant à l'égard de

unless à moins que... ne
unlock ouvrir
unmitigated fieffé (gredin), absolu...
unpack défaire ses bagages
unsealed non cacheté
unwillingly à contrecœur
unwise mal avisé
upper du haut
upright tout droit
upshot résultat, fin mot
upstairs en haut
upturn retourner
use employer
use utilité, usage
useless inutile, bon à rien
usually habituellement
usual (as) comme d'habitude
utter émettre (un mot)

— V —

valuable précieux
van camionnette
velvety de velours
viciously méchamment
vindictive rancunier
vine plant

— W —

wage salaire
wainscot lambris
wait attente
waiter garçon (de café)
wake, woke ou waked, woken se réveiller
walking privileges droit de circuler librement
walking-stick canne
wall mur
wall-eyed vairon
wander errer
wander about circuler librement
wanderer vagabond
war guerre
ward salle, pavillon (hôpital)
warm (ré)chauffer
warm chaleureux
wash laver

washing linge
waste paper basket corbeille à papier
watch montre
watch-chain chaîne de montre
water (make one's mouth) faire venir l'eau à la bouche
water-bottle bouillotte
watever tout ce que
wave vague
wave osciller
wave aside écarter de la main
way chemin, trajet
weak faible
weakness faiblesse
weapon arme
wear away, wore, worn passer lentement (temps)
wearily avec lassitude
wear, wore, worn porter (vêtements)
weaver tisserand
weeds mauvaises herbes
weep, wept, wept pleurer
weigh peser
welcome accueillir
welcoming accueillant
welfare bien-être
western de l'ouest
wet humide, mouillé
whale baleine
whenever chaque fois que
whether si
while pendant que
while espace de temps
whisper murmure
whistle siffler
whoever qui que ce soit
whole entier
why mais, oh !, eh bien
wicked méchant
wide large
wide open grand ouvert
widow veuve
wield manier, tenir
wife épouse

wild insensé, fou
wildly d'un air affolé
wind vent
window-frame montant de fenêtre
window-pane carreau
window-sill rebord de fenêtre
wing aile
wink at faire un clin d'œil à
wipe essuyer
wire fil (téléphonique)
wish désir
wistfully d'un air d'envie et de regret
within dans moins de
wonder merveille
wonder se demander
wonder over se poser des questions sur
wonderful magnifique
wonderingly avec étonnement
wood bois
woodwork boiserie
woollen en laine
word parole, mot
work marcher (machine)
workroom atelier
world monde
worn usé
worry souci
worth (doing...) qui mérite (d'être fait)
wretch scélérat
wretchedness misère, désarroi
wrinkle froncer, rider
wrist poignet
write, wrote, written écrire

— Y —

yard cour
yard 91.44 cm
yell hurler
yellow jaune
yellowed jauni
yet cependant

Imprimé en France sur Presse Offset par

BRODARD & TAUPIN

GROUPE CPI

La Flèche (Sarthe).
N° d'imprimeur : 12263 – Dépôt légal Édit. 19691-03/2002
LIBRAIRIE GÉNÉRALE FRANÇAISE - 43, quai de Grenelle - 75015 Paris.

ISBN : 2 - 253 - 04684 - 1   30/8600/6